A Charmed Life

☼

Dee Trainor

To Shirly,
Lets keep on
writing & painting
It's the good life!
With Warm Regards,
Dee

Copyright © 2013 by Dee Trainor

All rights reserved. No part of this book may be reproduced, stored, or transmitted by any means—whether auditory, graphic, mechanical, or electronic—without written permission of both publisher and author, except in the case of brief excerpts used in critical articles and reviews. Unauthorized reproduction of any part of this work is illegal and is punishable by law.

Printed and bound in the United States of America

This book or any part thereof, may not be reproduced for sale

Without written permission from the author

Lulu.com

ISBN 978-1-300-68714-6

Cover Illustration by Rebecca Feeney (granddaughter)

Table of Contents

Dedication 1
Introduction 2
Tea for Two 4
Pete's Travels 8
Tom's Accident 10
The Tooth Fairy 15
Pete's Story 18
Busted at the Dime Store 21
Ham and Cheese 24
Bonnie and Clyde 26
The Easter Bunny 30
Jack's Dream Car 33
Slow Burn 38
Motherhood 41
St. Vincent de Paul's Angels 43
A Charmed Life 46
My First Real Job and Community College 49
My New Life 51
Queen of Hearts 53
The Case of the Infamous Wedding Gown 56
Joan and Mike's Wedding 62
We Lose Mike 65
Joan's Pregnancy 69
Painting in Italy 72
Missing Mother Teresa 77

Mom's Last Day 81
Aeroplane Stories 86
BC # One 90
Good Bye Dad 93
Public Enemy Number One 96

Dedication

I dedicate this book to my children, they are the most outstanding people I have ever known, and I would trust any one of them with my soul.

From left: Carol, Tom, Pete, Jack, Dee, Joan, Barney, Sharon

Introduction

I have occasionally told my stories to family and friends, but the idea of publishing them for the world to read was never, ever in my plans. Any encouragement to do so was usually nixed by me—with the thought, *why would anyone want to read about my life?*

I've never been much of a reader let alone a writer; however, we all have our stories. If you're on this earth, and you've survived your childhood, you probably have a story or two to tell.

Well, the idea slowly fermented and I signed up for a writing class with Margo LaGutata, a Detroit Poet, and found that I had a lot to say. Each week we read a story and got feedback from the other participants, all constructive critique. My work was well received and after a few weeks she told me, "You have found your voice."

Over a number of years, I would write periodically, but never with much enthusiasm and definitely not with the intention of publishing. Then a few years ago, I joined a group led by Iris Underwood, a great Facilitator. Many people in the group had published and provided productive critiques. I learned a lot and was encouraged to continue writing. Later, I found a group at the Birmingham Senior Center with several people who had also published. My stories were well received, and I was further encouraged to collect my stories and put them in a book. Since then, I have been on a mission to complete it—off and on anyway, since that is how I do things. It took such discipline to keep at it, but here it is. I wanted to get it all down before I began forgetting, and at my age, that is a real possibility. When I first mentioned this to my family, I already had the title and about 25 topics that I wanted to write about. They asked, "What's the title Mom?" I said, "*A Charmed Life.*" They said, "What? If that was a charmed life, I'd hate to see a cursed one." I said, "I know a lot of bad things have happened, but I always came out of it OK." They said, "Mom, those stories took place a long time ago, and you're not a writer." I said, "I know, but I am going to preface the book by saying that most of these stories are about situations that took place during the last half of the 20th century, and they are written in the vernacular." Human interest stories don't have a timeframe, they are perpetually now. The cast of characters, along with me, are listed below in birth order:

Jack, Tom, Carol, Pete, Sharon, Barney, Joan

Oh, I should mention their father had not been with us since Jack was around twelve and Joan was a little over two.

I'm ordinarily a very private person. I worked as a Special Education Teacher for twenty-five years and most of my co-workers knew very little about me. However, sometimes in casual conversation little bits of info about my life would slip out. Except for my therapy group, I keep a pretty low profile. When people do hear little bits about my life they say, "You should write a book, Trainor." My brother says, "People won't believe it, but you should write it anyway." After I finally decided to document parts of my life, a voice in my head said, *that's the silliest thing I have ever heard, you can't write a book.* Then I realized that's not my voice, that's my mother's voice. Even though she's been gone since 2002, she was kind enough to leave me her critical voice to be sure I don't get, "too big for my britches," as she used to say. Then I talk right back to her and say, "Guess what, I can do this?" So I made a list of topics that I thought would be interesting. I just recounted my list of topics; can you believe I have 51? Although all of the topics are not covered in this First Edition, I plan to add them in the coming years—stay tuned.

Tea for Two

My Mom had this old photo album. The cover was black simulated leather that seemed to be made like filo dough. It seemed like someone took layers of thin paper, some of it even red, but mostly black, and pressed them together. The word "Photographs" was on the cover and you could tell that at one time it had been embossed in gold. It was held together with a worn black cord that went through two-punched holes at the end; that way you could add or remove pages as needed. There weren't plastic sleeves to slide the picture into in those days, of course, but she had a pack of little white corners that had to be glued on the paper to fit the size of the picture. Then you slid the picture under the corners—it was a lot of work. I know because that was my job licking and sticking. When I was younger, I used to look at the pictures and wonder how girls could swim with all those clothes on, plus a hat! There was one of my Grandma Carr standing next to Uncle Harold proudly wearing his WWI uniform. She's only forty-one years old, but she's wearing a long, black dress and her hair is tied back in a bun. She looks much older than a forty-one year old woman today. There are lots of pictures of my Mom and her girlfriends. They look so happy playing tennis or rowing a boat and laughing. She was very pretty. She had thick, wavy auburn hair, clear milky white skin, and pale blue eyes.

Typed on top of one photo were the words: *Belle Isle, Detroit, Michigan July 26, 1919*. There they were, Mom and Dad standing in front of the greenhouse in a loving embrace. Dad wore a black and white striped shirt, black pants, and black suspenders. Mom was wearing a long, white summer dress with a bow in the back. The skirt had tucks all the way down with a narrow ruffle about every seven inches. Dad had his left arm over her shoulder and around her back till it just touched his right arm. His right arm was under Moms and wrapped around till it rested over her backbone. Mom had her arms around Dad too with her hands clasped behind him at the waist. In a tight embrace, with cheeks pressed together, they smiled into the camera. Two love birds totally present in the moment.

But actually I don't know these two people. As far as I can remember, my Mom was always angry or in a bad mood. My Dad was fun and funny, but he was rarely at home. Maybe that was what she was always so angry about. I suppose when they got married they had all the hopes and dreams of every young couple, but something must have gone terribly wrong.

Looking back, my Mom did have a rather hard life. My parents built a two-family flat, piece by piece so that the money from the upstairs renters could pay half the mortgage. I was about two years old then; the first girl and I had six-year-old and six-month-old brothers.

My Dad worked for the Brach's Candy Company as a traveling salesman. He went out of town on Monday morning and didn't come home until Friday night which was usually when the *Lone Ranger* was on the radio. Maybe my Mom just got bitter because she had to: shovel the coal, empty the ashes, wash, iron, cook, and clean.

Eventually she had five children to take care of all week; and if there were any problems at school, or if anyone got sick or hurt, it was her responsibility. Also, if my Dad wasn't home when it was time to go to the hospital to deliver the babies, she had to call a neighbor to take her. She didn't have any family in Detroit; they were all in Fort Wayne, Indiana, her hometown. I'm sure she was lonely at times.

My Dad was always cheerful and fun. He enjoyed his children which probably wasn't too hard since he only had to see them on weekends. He was staying in a hotel and eating out at restaurants all week. He didn't have to put up with the bickering and quarreling or the discipline. When my Dad came home, he would toot the horn in front of the house and we would all run out and jump on the running board and get a ride up the driveway. I can still remember the thrill of that ride; my hair blowing in the wind and my skirt billowing out in back. I make it sound like he was going about thirty miles an hour; but when you are young and doing something dangerous and forbidden; everything takes on a mythical air. You're transported!

My Dad always had candy when he came home; from a kid's point of view, what a great Dad! From a wife's point of view, whatever happened to the *Tea for Two*? It must have been a crushing disappointment. I don't ever remember seeing my Mom and Dad kiss, hold hands or even exchange a loving glance. Even in my Dad's retirement years, my Mom never stopped nagging and discounting him. I remember how angry she got and how impatient she was when my Dad started to get senile and couldn't get his arm in his coat sleeve. I know how hurtful this was because I was also singled out to bear my Mom's wrath. My Dad and I always thought something terrible must have happened to my Mom when she was growing up to make her so angry with us.

Anyway, this story has a happy ending, believe it or not. My Mom moved to St. Anne's Mead nursing home about two years after my Dad passed away. In her final years, Mom still looked very beautiful with fluffy white hair, puffy pink cheeks, and hardly any wrinkles. She still had the same clear, blue eyes. She remained very smart, used the telephone, put her hearing aid battery in and used dental floss daily. People who came to visit her always remarked that she looked so good. Everyone loved her at "The Mead"—she was as sweet as pie. After being mean to me all those years, in the last four months at the Mead, she apparently forgot she didn't like me! She was even being sweet to me, and I was almost starting to like her. She had just turned 104 years old and I thought maybe we'll kiss and make up. Then I came to my senses and said (to myself), *Naah!*

Dee Trainor 7

Joe & Marie Smith

Pete's Travels

I'm sitting here watching Anderson Cooper on television. He's interviewing the family of a teenager who committed suicide as a result of being bullied in school. This makes me think of my son, Pete who was a special needs student. I wonder how many times he was bullied and teased that I never knew about. In those days, the derogatory word for people like Pete was "retard."

Pete didn't look different than anyone else and he wouldn't be picked out in a crowd; but during a conversation, it would become evident that he wasn't quite on track. He started kindergarten at Greenfield School in Birmingham when he was five years old, just like all the other kids. As time went on, we could see that he wasn't keeping up with his classmates. He couldn't seem to learn his colors, recognize numbers, or do any counting. When his teachers learned that Pete's Dad had left the family, they thought that was the problem. Also, I was told that boys were less mature and he would probably catch up later, but they decided that Pete should repeat kindergarten. One more year would make the difference. What was in Pete's favor was that he had good social skills, he was well behaved, and he wasn't a problem child. He knew how to take turns, share and follow directions. Thank you, Jesus for letting him grow-up in a large family where these skills are crucial for survival. Sharon, Pete's younger sister, was entering kindergarten the next year and Greenfield School had two kindergarten classes, so luckily Sharon and Pete could be in separate rooms.

The following year they were both off to first grade at Our Lady Queen of Martyrs, where they would join their three older siblings Jack, Tom, and Carol. However, that was the end of the line for Pete; it was at this point that I realized that there was no way that he could keep up. His sweet personality and charming ways were no match for the vigorous regimen of reading, writing, and mathematics demanded by the Nuns. Even in a class of thirty-five students, Pete stood out. After lots of meetings and testing (see other story about Pete), he ended up in the Special Education program in the Birmingham School District.

You may remember the way special education students were treated from your own grade school years. They were usually the last room at the end of the hall or near the janitor's closet—I wonder why that was. So, each morning while most of the kids were lining up on the corner waiting for the regular school bus, the small special education bus driven by Mr. Fosmo pulled up in front of our house. Imagine how humiliating that was for Pete, being a Special Ed child in our upper-middle-class Catholic ghetto, where the average IQ was around 120? Furthermore, the stigma of being a single mother of seven children didn't really endear us to the neighborhood either. We became interlopers in our own neighborhood but away from home, where people did not know us, it was a different story.

I remember one summer when we were at Camp Dearborn, a family camp located on a lake about 30 miles from our house. Pete was probably about nine years old, and on Wednesday nights they showed movies outside on the lawn. I was sitting in the back on a blanket with my youngest child, Joan. Pete was up front near Tom, his brother. Tom heard some kids talking to Pete, they were asking him some questions and he was giving all the wrong answers. So, Tom came back to tell me what was happening. Well, the cat was out of the bag and they began laughing and mimicking Pete. I told Tom to get Pete and to come back and sit with me. This was in the early sixties when *Father Knows Best* and *June Cleaver* where the idols. Over the years we were gradually accepted; and I believe that this was because my children stuck together, supported each other, and toughed it out.

I know I will not always be there to protect Pete, but thankfully he knows how to live in the world better than most—he is my hero!

Later in life, Pete married a classmate of his and of all my children, who do you think had twins? Right, Pete and Laura—their babies were 1 lb. 13 oz. and 1 lb. 14 oz. when they were born. But that's another story.

Tom's Accident

My granddaughter, Rebecca is helping edit my manuscript for me. We were both with Tom last week for a visit at the NJ shore and she spent time reading some of my stories. She said, "You don't have any stories about my Dad, Gramma." I said, "I guess I don't." Then, I remembered the worst tragedy that had befallen me and my family.

Tom and his friend, Brian were going uptown to the bowling alley for a game. It was a Saturday afternoon and I can remember the exact date, February 12th, Lincoln's birthday as a matter of fact, the year was 1964. I know this because Tom was 13 years old and he was born in 1950. He was in the eighth grade at Our Lady Queen of Martyrs. Isn't that funny how we put little facts together to jar our memories? I guess it was a regular Saturday, nothing remarkable going on, just the kids playing and watching TV. However, in the afternoon I got a call from Beaumont Hospital telling me that my son had been in an accident crossing Woodward, and was brought to the hospital in an ambulance.

I ran next door to my neighbor, Corkey. She had been our guardian angel many, many times. I banged on her back door, she opened the door and I just stood there looking at her. I couldn't speak. She said, "What is the matter?" I was finally able to get it out and she said, "Grab your coat; I am taking you to the hospital."

I guess she must have called my parents because my Dad arrived a few minutes later at the hospital. I was standing next to Tom laying on the gurney when our pediatrician came in the room. He looked Tom over; he actually did not look too bad and did not have any apparent injuries. "He seems to be congested, he must have a cold," said our pediatrician. I said, "No, he does not have a cold." The pediatrician patted him on the stomach a few times and said, "He is fine, just shaken up a little bit. You can take him home and let him get some rest tonight." Tom didn't seem like himself, he didn't say a word.

My Dad was with me, and as instructed by our pediatrician, we got Tom up. He was a little wobbly so we got a hold of him under each arm. We were trying to get him to walk, but with great difficulty. We were actually dragging him along the hospital halls. Before we got too far, another nurse came out and asked us, "Where are you going"? We said, "He has been discharged by the doctor and we are taking him back home." She said, "Wait a minute, I think we should check one more thing." She took him back into the room and they took a urine sample; it was nothing but blood.

Tom was immediately readmitted. He didn't have a cold as the doctor thought; instead his lungs were filling up with blood making him sound like he was congested. After a while, they told us (Dad and me) that we could go home. Tom would be staying overnight.

Recently, I ran across one of my Mom's journals and found the entry for that tragic day. She wrote, *Tommy Trainor was hit by a car today. Jack is so worried; he just walked the floor all night.* Remember, Jack was only 14 years old, but seemed so much older. Jack and Tom were the father figures for 5 younger siblings, so Jack knew if one was gone, (he or Tom) then the whole thing would fall apart and would ultimately fall on his shoulders.

Tom was found 100 feet from the point of impact; he had flown through the air when the car hit him. He was actually found in the median (island) in the middle of the road. He and Brian were trying to cross eight lanes of traffic, four in each direction. The trick was to see if you could cross all eight without stopping at the median in the middle. A diagonal street also cuts across the eight lanes and takes you into downtown. Apparently, the driver of the car was also trying to make all eight, so he ran the stop sign at the median (reported by Police). Brian saw him at the last minute and dove back to the median; he was clipped in the ankles (reported by Brian). Tom never saw the car and to this day has no memory of the impact. His last memory was bowling his high game that year, and telling Brian, "Let me carry the French fries when we run across the street because you might drop them."

My Dad dropped me off at my house and then he went home. I was standing in my closet putting on my pajamas and crying when the phone rang, "Mrs. Trainor, this is the nurse from Beaumont, you better come back, we don't know if your son Tom will make it through the night." I frantically dressed and called my Dad to come pick me up. When we arrived, Tom was in emergency surgery. His spleen had been smashed into pieces. He had a bruised kidney and bruised lungs, but thankfully he made it through surgery. However, the doctor said, "He is not out of the woods yet." We kept vigil all night.

Afterwards, they asked me if I wanted him to be sent to the children's section or the main ward of the hospital. I smiled when she asked about the children's section. Of course, Tom would be going to the main ward; I couldn't imagine him in the children's section. He was only thirteen, but I always thought he was grown-up. My Dad took me back to the hospital the next morning, my sister-in-law, Dee and my Mom came over to my house to straighten up and watch over the other kids. When I arrived at the hospital, Tom seemed okay; he didn't have any marks on his face or arms. He didn't look like he had been hit by a car unless you looked under his gown and saw a twelve-inch-long incision from the middle of his belly button to his side. Two days later when I came back, they were changing Tom's sheets and they noticed bloody bandages on his feet which were stuck to cuts which were now infected. The bandages were removed and the sores cleaned, but he still has scars in those areas. Ten days after the accident they decided that Tom should get up and walk around; but when he did, he complained that his right ankle hurt. They decided to do an X-ray and found that the ankle was broken, so they set it and put on a cast. Three days later they decided that Tom should try out crutches. As he was hopping around on the left leg, he reported that ankle also hurt. Another X-ray and, *yes,* the left ankle was also broken, but had already begun to heal. They decided not to re-break it, so Tom had to use a wheelchair until both legs healed.

One day when I was in Tom's hospital room, I went into the bathroom to cry. Dr. Dorsey came in and said, "Tom is going to be fine and it's okay to cry in the room." But for me, it wasn't okay to cry in front of Tom. I never wanted the kids to see me cry because I didn't want them to be scared. I always thought if I didn't say anything or show my true emotions, then the kids would think that everything was fine and they would keep going.

Before he finally went home, he also came down with pneumonia. Every day when I came home from the hospital, friends and family called to see how Tom was progressing. There was always a new medical problem to report. I was completely put out and I asked the doctors/nurses, "Why didn't you notice all these problems right away?" To think, if my Dad and I had dragged Tom out of the hospital with all those problems, he would have died on the way home. They replied in somber tones, "At first, we were just trying to keep him alive." He was so close to death they weren't concerned with the extremities. He was bedridden for a while; bed pans and washouts by a nurse. You can imagine how embarrassing that would be for a young, teenage boy.

Tom was in a room with three men, he was so sweet; the staff and everyone just loved him. When I came to visit, he would be smiling and joking. Then, he would say Mom, "Can you please close the curtains around the bed." I obeyed. Once the curtains were closed, he would grit his teeth; and in a threatening low voice say, "Get me out of here, Mom! I am not staying here." He was still bed ridden. I think in total, he was in the hospital for about three weeks. When he came home, he was confined to a wheelchair. Our carpeting had long since been relocated to the trash and there was a long hard-wood floor hall from the living room past the kitchen door and down to the bedrooms. It was about twelve-feet long and made a great race track. Tom would start at one end and tear down to the living room. There was a shelf there that the little kids used to knock down when running around the corner. When Tom was in his wheelchair, I just took it down—it was one of my favorite pieces. When we sold the Birwood home, the black tire marks were still on the floor.

Another one of his favorite tricks was to tear down the driveway to see if he could stop before going into the street. He soon graduated to crutches and eventually got rid of the cast on his leg and went back to school. He didn't have his picture in the 8th grade graduating class yearbook because he was in the hospital at the time the pictures were taken.

Tom had always been an active and energetic kid, always testing his limits and then setting new goals. He used to run down the hall and jump to see if he could touch the top of the archway, or you could find him standing on his head against the wall until he got steady enough without it. He was good at this next one, thank heavens. He would start in the dining room and take a short run, then do a handspring and stopped just short of the five-foot square picture window in the living room. All this was a precursor to his feats as an adult. He achieved a black belt in Tae Kwon Do, ran the NJ marathon and recently, he took part in a couple of triathlons. A swim down the Hudson River… "Yuck!" Then, get out of the water, run to meet a friend who brought his bike—ride to Philadelphia, carry the bike over a bridge, leave the bike and run the race to the finish line "Hurrah!"

Tom still keeps in shape. He loves to run, mountain bike, swim, kayak, and probably much more. He was always trying to get a "six pack." You know what that is? It's when all six abs stand out on your midsection. However, due to the lengthy scar from his spleenectomy, he can only get a 5-pack. Oh, poor fellow.

The Tooth Fairy

Remember the title of this book "*A Charmed Life*"? You probably didn't think I meant it literally, did you? Well, you would be wrong; we had so many miracles in those days you wouldn't believe it. The following story is an example of one such miracle that happened in 1967.

I had a very good dentist in Royal Oak whose name I got from my old babysitter. He was up on all the newest techniques, and it was my first experience with a dental chair that allowed the patients to lie back comfortably. I'm sure you've experienced them since all of the dentists have them now. Back in the day, the dentist chair was the same as a barber's chair. The only moving part, other than up and down, was the headrest which could tip back. So, in that chair you could have your teeth examined or get a shave. But today, most dentists use a chair that doubles for a lounge chair. They try to make you think you're going to just relax while someone has both hands in your mouth and is about to insert a metal drill. Just as an aside, this position, with a man's face hovering right over me, brought up buried memories; and I began to tremble and shake. Thereafter, dental visits required mild medications to keep me calm.

Eventually, I learned to trust this dentist over the span of a few years. I've always required a lot of dental work maybe because my Dad was employed by Brach's Candy Company his entire working life. Shortly after I started to feel comfortable with Dr. Eggelston, he informed me that he was giving up his practice and going into orthodontics!!! Help, what was I going to do? I knew it would be hard for me to find a dentist that I trusted and who would have patience with my anxiety.

My brother, Jack and his family had a dentist they liked very much, Dr. Eugene Pourcho. His practice was right on Woodward Avenue near the AAA office in Birmingham. I got his name and number and made an appointment for a checkup. My brother told Dr. Pourcho a little bit about me and my circumstances. He mentioned that I was a single mother attending school, raising my family alone, and that we were having a bit of a struggle making ends meet.

At my first appointment, I found him very gentle, patient, and understanding. I was put at ease as much as possible with my anxieties. I got in the chair; he laid it back and checked my teeth. He came across an old molar, the last one on the bottom left. It had an old filling and it had started to breakdown. I remember that tooth, I broke it while chewing on one of those little red hot candies years before. You know when you have a problem but you hope the dentist won't notice and you can get by a little longer?

After a thorough exam, Dr. Pourcho said, "Mrs. Trainor, you need a crown on that back molar." Then he turned away from me to retrieve an instrument from another tray. I took the bib off from around my neck and began to let my legs slide off the side of the chair. He turned, looked at me and said, "Where are you going?" I said, "Well, I don't have any money for that right now. I'll call back and make an appointment for another day." He put his hand on my shoulder, looked me straight in the eye and said, "Mrs. Trainor, let me give that to you." I was taken aback and said, "No, I couldn't let you do that", I was so embarrassed. He said, "I want to fix that tooth for you." I guess I said "okay", I don't remember, but I remember he took my hand and helped me back into the chair and started the preliminary steps. When I left, I said to the receptionist, (who happened to be his sister) "I can't let him do that for me, I feel awful." After sharing a little bit about his childhood, she said, "Let him do that for you, he wants to."

I stayed with Dr. Pourcho as my dentist for a long time; actually, until he retired. One of the things I loved about him, other than his manner and great skills, was that he put these large earphones on your head when you were ready to be worked on. You could choose the music you wanted and then turn the volume up as loud as you dared. I always chose Handel's *"Water Music."* I don't know why but it always seemed to do the trick. When that sound commenced, I was transported to another dimension and before I knew it, he was finished.

A number of years later I ran into him and another man at Metro Airport in Detroit. I recognized him immediately. He introduced me to his friend and then we had a little chat. I told him that I had a degree in education and was working as a special education teacher in Macomb County. He was delighted to hear that and said, "I knew you would make it through those hard times." I thanked him again for his kindness. They were off on their way to a remote outpost to deliver bibles to some unfortunate people.

When was the last time that a dentist gave you a gold crown free of charge? When my children were young and lost a tooth, they always expected the tooth fairy to visit our house and leave money under their pillow. It wasn't until years later that my tooth fairy came around. He was one of the most wonderful people I've ever met. He really lived his Christian faith. God Bless you, Dr. Pourcho, and thank you again.

PS: This story took place years ago, probably over 50 years anyway. I still have that gold crown. It's still as good as new, "Want to see?"

Pete's Story

Where do I start with Pete? I'll tell you one thing, if you're in a Euchre card-playing tournament, partner up with Pete. He's a whiz at cards. Pete is my fourth child and when he was two-and-a-half years old he had a younger brother and sister, two older brothers, and one older sister.

Pete seemed to follow the development pattern of the other kids, or maybe he just followed the other kids. He was very independent, walked, talked, learned to ride a two-wheeler, tie his shoes and dress himself like everyone else, I think! As I'm writing this, I'm aware that I don't really know all of those details—maybe the other kids helped him along.

I just called my daughter, Sharon who is a year younger than Pete and asked her some questions in an effort to try to piece together this puzzle. Then we started remembering some instances and then broke out in laughter. How did we survive? I do remember when they were in high school and in different buildings, Pete at Berkshire and Sharon at Groves, but they rode the same school bus. Sharon had a large group of friends and they really looked out for Pete. He didn't need a lot of looking after, but in those days, Special Ed kids were the targets of ridicule. They were called retards and made fun of, but Sharon and her "Gang" made sure that if anyone thought of teasing Pete, they would answer to her. She was tough! But Pete always knew how to handle himself. He knew when to make himself invisible and to joke his way out of things. Great coping skills!

When Pete was younger he was best friends with a very smart kid down the street. They got along famously but when they started to play Monopoly or other games, Pete made an excuse to go home. He didn't understand money and couldn't read, so he always figured a way to get out of uncomfortable situations. Pete wrote the book on finesse and tact, what a genius. But getting back to when he was younger.

One time, on a fine summer day, Sharon and Pete then two and three years old walked into a neighbor's open front door, climbed up on a chair and let their bird out of the cage, then left. Another time, (I thought I'd go to prison for this one) they went into a neighbor's house, a different neighbor this time, and collected their mail out of the mailbox and brought it home to me. This neighbor was really furious, as this was a federal offense. He made all kinds of threats—one just short of double vivisection—or counting me—a triple vivisection. Then, there was the time they got the hose and sent a gentle spray into the dining room window of the house next door. Sharon and Pete were two sweet little children, one cuter than the other; however, they were adventurous and curious. The real problem was that they weren't really supervised very well. When we moved from Birmingham to Beverly Hills, Pete had just turned five, and I was a couple of months away from delivering our seventh child, Joan.

Pete went to kindergarten at Greenfield School, but he didn't seem to be keeping up with the other children. At a parent conference near the end of the term, the teacher recommended he repeat this class. I was afraid this would be a problem because Sharon was starting kindergarten the next year. She assured me they could be in different classrooms, "I guess it will all work out," I said. During Pete's second time around in kindergarten, he was still not getting it, and the teacher asked me if I could work with him for just an hour a night to help him along. We were all trying to drill him on his colors and numbers recognition, but it never seemed to sink in.

About this time, the children's father and I separated; they didn't call it that in those days, but that was the explanation for any and all of the problems. We had a "dysfunctional family" no need to look further. The next September, Pete and Sharon joined the other children at Our Lady Queen of Martyrs School and that was a BIG mistake.

The Nuns had little patience for a child with an IQ of less than one hundred and fifteen, and with thirty students in a class, Pete fell through the cracks. Finally, they suggested I take him to a Sister Mary at Marygrove University. She was a renowned-reading specialist; and if anyone could help Pete, it was her. She gave him a battery of tests, and concluded that he was just immature, "Boys always are", she claimed. Considering our family situation, she thought he would catch up in time.

We were all struggling, when a neighbor who had been a teacher in the school system, suggested I take Pete to the Birmingham Board of Education and have him tested again. This was radical thinking because we were CATHOLIC! All of our families were educated in CATHOLIC schools—from first to twelfth grade. All our cousins were at Catholic schools and the older children were there and doing well. How could we consider going to a public school? Not knowing where else to turn, I made an appointment and Pete was given another battery of tests. I was also asked to take him to a clinic for an EEG; I didn't even know what an EEG was. What happens is they put some material like Vaseline on your scalp in various places, and then they attach the electrodes to the Vaseline. Then the wires were attached to a machine that measures brain waves. Even though I was terrified, my usual Modus Operandi was, *if I don't make a big deal out of it, if I seemed OK with it, the kids would assume everything was all right and not to worry.* This is something I feel so bad about now. My poor kids never knew what was going on. I didn't know how to explain things because I didn't understand them myself.

After all the data was collected and completed, I received a call to come to the Board of Education for the results. When I arrived, I was ushered into the office of "Mr. M", Director of Special Education. This still didn't register with me as I sat across from a desk that had a few piles of papers here and there. The face behind the desk was round and quite ruddy with rather thick horn-rimmed glasses, thinning brown, grey hair, and a mouth that turned down at each corner. He stood up and stared at me not saying a word; then in a loud demeaning voice, he said, "Your kid is retarded. Why didn't you bring him in years ago?" I froze. Total guilt and shame gripped my body. I didn't know what to say. I think I asked him what he meant when he said something about Pete being "just the garden variety." He said, "There's no specific cause for his retardation, it is not genetic or the results of any trauma. It just happens, like in a field of daisies, where one dandelion pops up."

Busted at the Dime Store

My daughter, Sharon was around eleven years old when we were on one of our shopping trips uptown. It must have been to get a last-minute gift because it was Christmas Eve. Well, there we were walking up and down the aisles of the local dime store.

They don't call them dime stores any more obviously; what could you possibly expect to find for a dime? Now we think the dollar store is a bargain! They never should have changed those stores; everything was right out in front of you. You could pick things up, look them over, and then return them to the counter between the glass dividers. Nowadays, you can't actually get to the merchandise because it is packaged so tightly you need a crowbar to open it. Do you remember "Evening in Paris" perfume? It came in a cobalt blue bottle that was sort of flat and round with a silver label. It always seemed to be the perfect Christmas gift for your mother. Either perfume or one of those little china figurines made in Japan. This dime store not only carried your last-minute gift but you could get a drink, a sandwich, and a sundae at the counter. You could even get (my favorite) a banana split. Only people who lived during this time period know what I'm talking about.

Anyway, back to the adventure. Sharon and I were walking around the notions counter, past the garter belts, bras, down the aisle with the patterns, knitting needles and yarn. We were walking down the old wooden floors and looking up occasionally, when I noticed some women clearing away from a small man wearing a worn hunting jacket. You know those black and red plaid ones? Some of the women had startled looks on their faces, their eyebrows were up, and their mouths were open. They were walking away fast while glancing back over their shoulders. Of course, I couldn't leave well enough alone; I had to find out what was going on, so I said to Sharon, "Let's go down aisle four." As we sauntered past the hairnets and bobby pins, the "hunter" was coming towards us. As we approached each other, I noticed he had his hands in his side pockets; and as we got closer, he made a motion that opened the front of his pants and lo and behold, jutting out of his opened zipper was a bluish, pink "unmentionable." If Mae West was there she would have opined that he was happy to see us. Well, I was as shocked as everyone else and there was innocent Sharon staring at a last-minute item that was not on our list. If Sharon had still been in the "Santa" years, I might have told her that the man had stolen Rudolph's red nose and hidden it in his pants—after all it was Christmas Eve. Instead, I said, "Sharon, don't look, follow me." We immediately went to the salesgirl at the counter closest to us and asked her to get the Manager. He came up to me with a puzzled look, and I explained what was going on and what I had seen. I was embarrassed and stumbled over unfamiliar words, but he got the drift of what I was trying to tell him. He slowly turned and saw the perpetrator just standing alone in the aisle. He started towards him trying to look casual; and as he got a little closer, his eyebrows went up and his jaw went down. He turned on his heels and immediately called the police who arrived in minutes. An officer approached the perpetrator, took him by the arm, and ushered him into the back seat of a waiting police car. He was very docile and went quietly. Another officer walked up to the Manager, they exchanged muffled words, and then they both silently and simultaneously looked at me. Again, I had to explain exactly what I saw—how embarrassing! The policeman took detailed notes along with my name, address and phone number. He thanked me very much for doing my civic duty.

Here we were again, Sharon and I, some of the first to experience the real world protruding into the sacred environs of Birmingham, Michigan. We immediately got into the car and went home. As we entered the front door, Sharon began to excitedly relate the whole story. All the children listened with eyebrows up and mouths open; they were totally shocked that a pervert was in our town— impossible.

After dinner, we all settled down in the living room watching (my favorite) *Perry Como* when the phone rang. It was the police. The officer asked me if I could come down to the station and identify the suspect. I got back in the car and went back uptown trying not to think too much about the incident. I found a parking place on the street and walked across the grass, up the stairs and pushed open the thick, heavy oak door to the building. A detective was waiting for me. He led me down a long hall and we turned left into another hall. Then we came to the interrogation room (I recognized it from the detective shows on TV).

They asked me to look through the window in the door. They said it was a one-way glass so I didn't have to worry that he could see me. The window was about five feet high, too high for me to see in, so they got me a stool. I saw a young man sitting on a wooden bench; he wore glasses, and had short light hair. He was sort of leaning over with his arms resting on his knees and looking at the tiled floor. I said to the officer, "Yes, that's the man." I felt like Judas betraying someone. They said, "We know him, he's been here before, he's about thirty-one years old, married, and has a couple of small kids." I said, "oh no." My heart dropped and I felt so sick to my stomach that I just stared at them. They helped me off the stool, I couldn't say a word. They requested my signature, thanked me and held the door open to the street as I left. Christmas Carols could be heard all over town and the big tree on the front lawn of the municipal building gleamed with colored lights. Blinking, I could hardly hold back the tears as I opened the car door. Driving home down Pierce Street, past all the decorated homes of the beautiful people, I was just devastated. Here it was Christmas Eve and some little children were waiting for their Dad to come home and help hang up their stockings. They didn't know he would not be coming home that night.

At our home, we were all feeling grateful for our many blessings, but somehow that incident cast a cloud over our joy and made it a rather sad *Silent Night*. I realized that the tears were also for my own little children because their Dad wasn't coming home to help them hang their stockings either.

Ham and Cheese

It's nice out here on the deck—a gentle breeze is stirring up the ninety-degree temperature. I just have time for lunch before I have to leave for an appointment so I made myself this great sandwich. Thick bread, sweet ham slices and melted cheese. I put some hot mustard on it to give it a little zip. You know the kind with the little brown specks in it? It's the poor man's *Grey Poupon*. I'm having pretzels too; I like to have something crunchy with a meal. There is something satisfying and vengeful about that crunch.

    I remembered that my Dad used to like ham sandwiches and when my Dad got older, he always wanted to get the "kids" together for lunch. That meant going out with my three brothers and me to Mavericks, a bar up on Woodward Avenue. My Dad always wanted a large, frosty glass of cold beer with a big head on it. That meant having an inch of white foam on top and some running down the sides, which seemed to be a sign of camaraderie or belonging, or having arrived. I'm not sure what, but it was special. When we were together, we always had lots of fun laughing and talking. He was so proud to be with his handsome, successful sons. My Dad was a good provider but he never felt that he moved out of his class. He was a respectable middle-class man. He and Mom would occasionally go out for lunch—but that meant Arby's or the Beef Carver—never a bar.

    My oldest brother, Dick was the star of the family who always entertained us with stories about his skiing escapades up north. He knows the owners of the ski lodges in northern Michigan and he would tell harrowing tales of snowmobile chases.

    My middle brother, Jack is so sweet. He is the father of six boys and they are all professionals. I was telling him that I was starting to do some writing. Well, trying to, that is. He said that his sister-in-law had been writing poetry for years and had just published another book. Wow!

Then, there's my baby brother, Joe with his furniture business. "Still the number one tennis player at the club—Joe?" I asked. I always like to tease him. My mother's right, they all look like they just stepped out of a bandbox. They are each as neat as a pin and with every hair in place all handsome and smart to boot. I was proud to be with them and my cute little Dad.

After the grand affair, I took my Dad home. I helped him up the stairs and into the kitchen. He seemed so content and pleased. He went into the TV room, turned on the set and relaxed into his easy chair which had an ottoman, of course. My Mom was at the kitchen table writing in her steno pad, that's her journal. She records every detail of every day's events so I leaned over her shoulder to read. *Dad went out to lunch with the boys, a great day.* Mom, I offered, "I was there too." She gave me that familiar dismissive shrug of the shoulders and snickered, "oh well."

Well, look at the time? I had better get going or I'll be late for my appointment. Speaking of lunch, that was a great sandwich I made for myself, all that thick ham and cheese, but you know, I still feel hungry. I'm so silly. What's the matter with me anyway?

Bonnie and Clyde

If you looked at me, I am sure you would see a sweet grandmotherly little woman. Even in my prime at 5' 1' tall, I was never an imposing figure. You wouldn't think I had been involved with the police would you? Well, I was in a major way! Two times!

The second encounter took place one winter evening shortly after Christmas. My daughter, Sharon and her life-long friend Peggy, both around twelve years old and I went uptown shopping. We had just made it into Himelhoch's, a Department Store in Birmingham, Michigan about fifteen minutes before closing. I do not remember why we were at this store. It was an upscale store that was out of our class in those days. We were usually Kaybaum's regulars, which was top of the line for us.

We were dressed casually in jeans, snow boots and pea coats—nothing special. However, Peggy was wearing her most prized Christmas gift, a bright red hat, sort of a beret with red matching mittens. They were what we would term "fire-engine red." She was a pretty girl with long blond hair, a turned-up nose, blue eyes and naturally rosy lips, though she was on the quiet side. Sharon was very pretty also, with light brown curly hair and a ready smile. She was more adventurous and outgoing than Peggy.

When you walked through the front door at Himelhoch's, you were in the center of the store. To the left were cosmetics, bath powder, perfume and the like. Further to the left were gloves and purses. If you turned down that aisle, you would be in "better dresses" in the back of the store. To the left of us, on the other side of the store, was the coat department where there were beautiful houndstooth plaid wools, a long pink leather swing coat, Chesterfields, and especially the Alpaca cashmeres. Wow! Then there were the furs, sleek orange and black leopard coats and sheared beaver with rhinestone buttons. In many of them, you could see the shiny gray satin linings. As we walked through, we were trying to act as though we belonged there.

Then we noticed an African American couple sauntering around the racks of fur coats; it caught our attention because it was unusual to see "blacks" in the suburbs in those days. They were a most-handsome couple but still seemed out of place. She was tall and slim wearing a purple crepe wrap-around dress caught up at the hip with a silver buckle. With her chin tipped up, she could look down over her high cheekbones and appraise the merchandise. We were apparently the only customers left in the store.

Her companion stood patiently off to one side. He was equally as tall and slim and just as good looking. The light shade of his camel coat made his mahogany features even more striking. The matronly saleswoman stood by and smiled with her head cocked to one side, her hands clasped together in front of her plaid pleated skirt—obviously, hoping for a sale. The customer tried on a silver fox coat and preened in front of the three-way mirror holding the generous collar up close to her ears. She turned and slowly looked back over her shoulder and admired the image gracing the glass. Then, she slipped out of the coat with her companion's help and draped it over his arm. She wanted to try on just one more coat before making a decision. This one was a gorgeous full length black diamond mink. The image brought a gleam to her eye and caused the corners of her mouth to curl up slightly. This was the one!

We were just completing our purchase and watching without watching, the scene about twenty feet to our right (we did not want to be so provincial as to stare). Just as I zipped my purse, the sales clerk screamed, "Stop, Help, Police." We turned to see the distinguished looking couple high tailing it out the front door. She was wearing the mink and he was carrying the fox. Animal rights were not an issue in those days so it is unlikely that this was a cruelty to animals' protest. They ran straight down Bates Street, alongside Kresge's, an alley ran behind it that came out on Henrietta Street. Do not even ask me how I knew this, but I said, "I'll bet they are going through the alley— come on girls, we can head them off." To this day, I have no idea what "head them off," meant. This was either a misplaced sense of the good guys always win, or I had been watching too much *Dragnet* (the *CSI* of the 60's). The girl's eyes were as big as saucers and their mouths hung open in disbelief, but they blindly obeyed the command. We flew down Maple, past Mitzelfield's, Grinnell's, and Sherman Shoes. They all became a blur as we streaked by. We tore across at Henrietta and just as we approached the alley, unbelievably, they burst forth. We almost crashed into them; we were within four feet of the perpetrators when we stopped on a dime. We were breathless, our chests were heaving up and down, but we tried to act casual like we had been standing there for hours. Right next to us by the curb was a black car with the doors wide open. Phase one of "head them off" plan worked great, but now the kids were terrified and Phase two of the plan was escaping me. Sharon has always had a brilliant memory for numbers even when in shock. I think even today she can recall the phone numbers of every friend she ever had. Anyway, the couple and the coats disappeared into the back seat of the car, the door slammed and the wheels squealed. Sharon said, "What should we do?" I whispered, "Get the license plate number." Sharon tried to be casual about looking at the number and committing it to memory. There were all kinds of commotion in town and everyone was asking what had happened. Who did what? Did they get away, etc? Of course, we knew. We were eyewitnesses to the whole crime from the beginning to the end.

Sharon was shaking and Peggy was crying; they just stood there stunned looking at me. Now what? As Hardy would have said to Laurel, "Another fine mess you've gotten me into." I had a cool head, my typical behavior in a crisis (being a Mom, you get a lot of practice doing that). Nevertheless, I must say, I was a bit shaken up myself.

I said, "We'll go to the police station and report everything that happened and give them the license plate number so they can trace the criminals." We gave the police the information along with our names and addresses and an accurate account of the robbery and our quick action. The police were very grateful and appreciative of our thinking and quick wit. As we drove home, we kept rehashing with disbelief, our experience. We then started reviewing and analyzing their every move. In retrospect, we knew there was something suspicious about them all along! When we got home, Peggy was still crying as she and Sharon were retelling the tale to the rest of the family. Peggy took off her treasured hat and mittens and vowed never to wear them again. She was convinced the criminals had seen her and would remember the girl in the red hat. She was convinced they would come back looking for her and silence her so that she could not testify against them. Again, too much *Dragnet*.

I went back to the police station a couple of weeks later to inquire about the case. They said thanks to our quick thinking and getting the license number of the getaway car, they were able to apprehend the criminals. They had been trying to get a break on this case for a long time, and apparently this led to the breakup of a ring of thieves who were responsible for other robberies (I love it when a plan comes together). You wonder how I could run so fast. Remember, these are tales from the twentieth century. However, I do not think contributing to the public safety of my community has gone unnoticed. When I am out walking in the neighborhood and a police car goes by, I see them nod at me, and then I know the story of my bravery and courage is still being told (Five-Foot Female Foils the Filchers) or (Minute Mother out Matches Mink Mobsters) or (Terrified Teen Refuses to Wear Red Hat). Ordinarily, I never get involved with the police, unless I am getting another speeding ticket.

The Easter Bunny

I believe I had a charmed life, but I think it was a nightmare for my kids. Hardship and uncertainty were ever present, but I never once heard anyone of them complain. I still feel so bad for them, they deserved better.

Especially Jack and Tom, they had to assume the role of Dad too often. Taking care of problems and trying to fix everything. They were just kids themselves but they always seemed so grown up and responsible. I'm amazed they never ran away; maybe they wanted to, but their loyalty to me and the family always won the day.

Today, when I see kids that age, there's no way they could have taken on that much responsibility. I remember one time when Jack was around eleven and Tom was around ten we were coloring eggs because it was a couple of days before Easter. That was always a big deal and a big mess. We had the newspapers spread out on the kitchen table—blue eggs, pink eggs, and green ones too.

You had to bend the little wire egg holder just right so the egg wouldn't fall through, that was the first challenge. Then, carefully put several drops of different oil color into the cup of hot water with some vinegar. Remember how this just seemed to spread a film of rainbow color over the surface? Then, just gently lower the egg till it was submerged, and finally slowly raise it up out of the water letting it dry on the empty egg carton. Walla, what a masterpiece!

You can see what a delicate procedure that was, so you can imagine fourteen little hands all wanting a turn. There was another older method my Mom told us about that she used when she was a girl. During her childhood, they didn't have dying kits, they made their own colors by boiling the brown skins of onions, or they used the water from boiling beets. They dipped the top half of the egg in one concoction and the bottom half in the other—it was a very smart combo.

The kids were intrigued so they had to try it themselves. Any rabbit would be proud to deliver eggs like these. Anyway, after boiling, cooling, and coloring the eggs, the kids were worn out. But wait, that's not quite right, I was worn out.

After washing hands and faces and brushing their teeth, they were off to bed. The Easter Bunny was coming tonight. So all off to bed except Jack and Tom, of course, they were the big kids. Dad will be here soon and we'll get the baskets down, fill them with goodies and hide the eggs. Waiting, waiting, waiting, I guess he's not coming, again.

Finally, about twelve in the morning Jack and Tom go outside to the backyard to bring the ladder in and set it up quietly in the hallway. The Easter baskets, along with the Christmas decorations, Halloween costumes, other holiday paraphernalia, like my old wedding dress were stored in the attic. To gain access to the attic opening, you had to climb the ladder, press your upper back, neck and shoulders against the 3ft. x 3ft. plywood cover; and at the same time, keep the palms of your hands pressed on each side to raise it evenly. If it wasn't kept even, it was in danger of tipping, falling through, and crashing to the floor. Tom held the ladder and Jack, the bigger and stronger by one year, climbed the ladder, raised the cover, and slid it over on to the rafters.

Tom followed with the flashlight and down below I reminded them not to trip on the beams, and stay on the ceiling boards, so as not to come through the ceiling. They each hiked themselves up and through the opening and scurried around till they found all seven little baskets with the green waxy grass still in from last year. They were talking in muffled tones so they would not wake the little kids. This was serious business like undertaking a clandestine coup.

I waited below holding the ladder and collecting each precious basket as it was handed down to me. Everyone knew their own basket. They were used year after year—it was tradition. Eventually, when they moved out or got married, I gave them their own basket to keep. "OK, that's it—be careful coming down" (it's always easier going up), I said. To get down you have to go backwards. First, lie on your stomach and let your legs hang over and then slowly lower yourself down until your feet touch the top of the ladder. Tom was first and Jack had to be last so that he could get a grip on the edge of the plywood cover and hike it into place. "Shhhh, be very quiet taking the ladder outside. Remember the kids think the Easter Bunny is performing all of this magic," I would whisper.

Jack and Tom got busy and filled the baskets with jelly beans, marshmallow chickens and chocolate rabbits; then, the most important part, hiding the baskets and colored eggs. I couldn't believe how creative they were. They were totally into it. One egg inside a half-closed book and another perched on the top of a lamp shade. One basket behind the curtain, one under the footstool and don't forget to look between the cushions of the couch. Don't forget they had to "hide" their own baskets or the whole charade would be exposed. Finally finished, they took their job very, very seriously, and now their time for bed, they looked so proud and satisfied with themselves.

Now it's the crack of dawn and I hear whispers and little feet scurrying around. As I enter the living room, I see that the big hunt is on. First, they must find their baskets and then hunt for the eggs.

Did Jack and Tom count the number of eggs they had hidden? Is the Pope Catholic? If someone was stumped, Tom would help out by giving clues. Example: "You're getting warm, you're getting warmer!", or "No, you're getting cold." These were clues to help the hunter discover the coveted prize. That was fun.

"Hey, here comes Dad down the hallway, I didn't even know he was home. I didn't even hear him come in last night, did you?" little voices were clamoring. "Dad, look what the Easter Bunny brought me!"

Jack and Tom looked at each other with sly smiles. They were so proud and pleased with themselves. But wait, something's wrong with this picture!

Jack's Dream Car

When Jack was still in high school, he had the usual array of junk cars. This is the way it was in the sixties. Kids did not get new cars in those days. After they learned how to drive, they usually got some old junker. They knew how to get them running because they liked working on them. Back then, when you opened the hood, you could actually identify the engine parts. There's the six spark plugs wired to the battery, the carburetor, the oil dipstick, an air filter, etc. Be sure to keep the water in the radiator so the engine won't overheat and so on.

Knowing your engine and the ability to keep it in good shape was sort of a status symbol or an adolescent rite of passage, you might say. In addition, in those days, kids could get jobs, save up some money and buy their own car. And that's the way it was at our house, especially under our circumstances.

Jack had always wanted a 1963 Ford Galaxy. That was his dream car. It was a miracle that he even got it because at the time he was saving for his car, he was also paying his high school tuition at Brother Rice, buying his own clothes, and paying for any other expenses he had. This was his long-awaited dream.

On any given day at 16027 Birwood, you could find a couple or more cars parked in the driveway. If you were number one and you wanted to get your car out, you would have to move car number two to the street, park it, then go back, get in car number one, reverse down the driveway, position car number one at the curb, get in car number two, shift gears, and drive back up into driveway. The procedure was repeated until the desired car was in the street and ready to go.

One day, Carol and her friend Gail wanted to move Jack's car so they could get Carol's car out to go shopping. They climbed into Jack's "new" car and turned the key and stepped on the gas pedal. The engine turned over but it wouldn't start. Whrrr, whrrr, pump the gas pedal, maybe it just needs to be primed, whrr, pump, whrrr, pump. Is it flooded? Of course, the brake was off and the car begins to roll down the driveway and out into the street. It didn't stop until it came to rest on the other side of the road next to the curb. Thanks to our *Charmed Life* status there wasn't another car coming down the street at that time, or God forbid, a child riding their bike on the sidewalk in front of our house. Gail tried starting the car again, no dice. I came out and tried it again. Then, while looking at the hood of the car, I noticed the beautiful green paint was beginning to develop small bubbles, then larger and larger ones. Oh my God, the car's on fire! I yelled, "Get out of the car and call the fire department." We jumped out of the car and ran across the street and stood on the front lawn. We were scared to death. The rest of the kids came out of the house and watched from the porch. When the fire engine wailed down the street with lights flashing, most of the neighborhood showed up. Everyone was standing around waiting and watching as the flames came licking out from under the front wheel wells. The horn was honking, an SOS signal while smoke came out of the windows. Was it going to blow up and explode? Oh my God, what have we done? We stood there terrified. The fireman just calmly hosed down the burning hulk. That was it—it was over. The cremation lasted only about 26 minutes. The end of the dream; and of course, the end of the money spent on the car. Both were gone.

Unfortunately, Jack hadn't purchased insurance on the car yet because he had just gotten it. And to add insult to injury, he later had to pay to have the carcass hauled away. We all just stood there crying, looking at each other and looking at Jack's precious car. Carol was horrified and overcome with guilt. We didn't know what to do.

Jack was always easy going. He never got rattled or upset. He could always take charge and fix everything. He was the oldest of the children. I guess you could say he was a surrogate Dad even though he wasn't even 18 years old yet. All the years that he lived at home, when he came home late from a date or a night out with the boys, no matter what hour, he always went to each bed to see if the assigned occupant was there. Then he would look into my room and say, "Mom, I'm home." If necessary, he would ask where the missing sibling was, "Was Sharon sleeping over at Peggy's house? Who is that in there with Barney?" After he checked to see that all was well with the family, he would go to bed himself.

We were all sitting around in the living room waiting for Jack to come home. We were so scared. What would he do? What would he say? His car was his pride and joy. He worked so hard to save his money and all for naught. How could he bear this news? Our hearts were breaking for him.

When he came home and we told him what happened, he didn't say a word. He went downstairs where he and the other boys had their bedroom. We didn't hear a sound, then finally a heavy thud. Later, we discovered he had punched a hole through the drywall.

The next morning everything went on as usual. The incident was never mentioned. I don't know how he kept from running away all those years. What a burden for a young teenage boy, the oldest of seven siblings. There always seemed to be a crisis and we always looked to Jack. He always seemed to have a solution.

That's the meaning of FAMILY and somehow we all survived. But, that's not the end of the story. This incident took place around the end of May and Brother Rice was gearing up for their annual Spring Fair. The Fair was a fundraiser. They were going to use the proceeds to replenish some football equipment: helmets, shoulder pads, and other things like that. One of the venues offered an opportunity to vent your primal rage by smashing up an old car. For a fee, of course! Jack donated his other old car, one that died a natural death about a month before. How heartbreaking that must have been for him. Dream, plan, work, save, and for what? This!

The Fair was crowded with families, young couples, school staff, and students. They had fishponds for the little ones, darts to throw at balloons, or you could try your luck by throwing a baseball knocking down some wooden milk bottles to win a stuffed bear. People were milling around laughing and having a good time and eating hot dogs, of course.

Then, you could hear a barker calling, "Give the man a dollar and you can take three swings with this sledge hammer at this old Chevy." The boys were lined up to test their strength and show off. Smash went the windshield; another blow sheared off the side-view mirror. A double dent to the hood! "Stand on the roof and get the back window out boys," shouted the barker. Wow! What fun! Thud, wham, bang, screech, clang, within a few hours the poor car was heaving its last breath. Now this was a moneymaker! Later they came and hauled it away. How heartbreaking that must have been for Jack, two cars within a month.

But before this happened, because we had donated the car, The Brother Rice Mother's Club wanted the photographer from the Birmingham Eccentric to come over and take our pictures so the paper could advertise the Fair. *My God, my God, why hast thou forsaken me?*

We had been alone for about six years at this point and everything was worn out and broken by then (including me). The springs on the couch were starting to make their appearance. The long, shag rug was way past its expiration date. The shelf in the living room had been knocked off so many times by little kids running around the corner that it had multiple scars imbedded in the wood. As often as I vacuumed, I still found dog hair, cat hair, hamster hair, bird feathers, a little grass left from the past Easter baskets, and usually a strand or two of tinsel from last year's Christmas tree.

None of the jelly jar glasses matched but neither did the dishes or silverware. The only thing that was intact was my precious family. *Thank you, Jesus!* Well, as many excuses as I made to try and discourage the mothers from coming to our house, they had a rebuttal. They were determined to honor us with their presence and take some pictures while we were "making cookies." Like I said, everything at our house was in disrepair due to lack of time and money, and the oven was no exception. It was the oven door. You had to know just how to open it—raise it up, put your foot under the door, press in, and then slowly lower it down. But you still had to hang onto the door. And don't move the foot either. Even if it was heavy or hot, just hold on; if you didn't, the door fell off. You know the glass window in the oven door? Ours was orange with dark, brown streaks baked on. You couldn't see through it if your life depended on it. And then if the oven was hot, a small puff of smoke made its escape when you opened the door. Cleaning the oven was way down on the list of things to do. It was probably twenty-one on a list of twenty. About four little Moms turned out. They looked like they had part-time jobs on *Father Knows Best*, a television show. Another woman was a ringer for June Cleaver. All my kids were in the hall peaking around the corner giggling.

But it all worked out. We didn't really make cookies, we were just pretending for the camera. And I made sure I was the one to open the door. I held it with a very large pot holder that sort of covered the oven window. Then, we were directed to smile at the camera and say, "cheese." After the bright flash, we took off our aprons with the little bows on the back. The Moms graciously thanked me for letting them use our kitchen to plug The Brother Rice High School Fling. They invited me to join the group, but that wasn't in the cards for me at that time in my life. It probably wouldn't be that way today either.

Slow Burn
(Buttering up the in-laws)

As I look over the list of topics that I want to write about, I see that most are loaded with emotions. Some evoke sadness, some happy times and some recall just plain anger and frustration. I guess that's life. The human condition! This falls into the latter category.

This situation took place when Pete was about 16 years old. Pete always liked to work around cars so he got a job at a gas station up on Woodward. This was at a time when kids could get odd jobs. You probably remember where you worked when you were in your teens.

About this time, my second oldest son, Tom got engaged to Patty Heathfield. They had both graduated from Michigan State University the year before and were living in Indiana where Tom got his first job. Incidentally, I graduated from MSU with them. I got a late start!

Patty's family, her Mom, Dad, and uncle lived not far from me in Rosedale Park in Detroit. Having a daughter-in-law from an extended family, I thought would bode well for me. You never know when you may need to move in with relatives.

I had been invited to their home a couple of times for social gatherings when Tom and Patty came home. We also had a couple of mutual high-school acquaintances. I thought I should have them over for dinner to reciprocate, and become better acquainted before the wedding festivities began that summer.

This was a big deal for me. I was a single-working Mom and I still had kids at home. So, my lifestyle was quite a contrast from theirs. If you read some of my stories, you will remember our house. It was even more worn out than before, and our oven door happened to be broken.

On the designated evening, I was scrambling around trying to pick up the house, set the table, and cook dinner. I decided to serve meatloaf and baked potatoes. I'm not much of a cook and I didn't think I could mess up a simple meal like that—an oven meal that could be put on about an hour before company arrived.

About twenty minutes before the guests were to arrive Pete came in waddling like a duck looking pale and scared. I said, "What are you doing home so early? You don't usually get home until about 8:30." He said, "Mom, I got burned."

I looked at him. He looked OK to me except that his pants were a little scorched on the inner thigh and he smelled like gasoline. Not unusual when you work at a gas station. In those days the attendant pumped the gas for the customers. Remember that?

I didn't see any damage. I thought Pete was exaggerating. Maybe someone threw a cigarette at him and he got scared. Some people think it's funny to tease people like Pete.

Anyway, I told Pete to go to the bathroom and take his pants off. I filled the tub about 1/3 the way up with cold water. I knew that was the new way to treat burns. The cold water would stop the burn from going deeper into the tissue. Remember when they use to put butter on to cool off the affected area? Later they learned that made it worse.

I told Pete to get into the tub and just stay there a little while. Of course, we only had one bathroom. I hoped no one needed to use it. When Pete took off his pants, I could see the inner thighs of both legs were scarlet and starting to blister. Just then, of course, the doorbell rang and in marched the three Heathfield's. I explained what had happened and said not to worry. I had everything under control. A barefaced lie!

I suggested Bob, Patty's Dad and Dick, her Uncle go into the living room and that dinner would be ready soon. "Make yourselves comfortable while I get you something to drink," I said. Actually, I was the one that needed a drink.

Patty's Mom, Catherine, came with me to check on Pete who was sitting in the tub of cold water. Poor Pete, it was humiliating enough for me to see him in his jockey shorts but now a complete stranger! Think of when you were sixteen? Catherine proceeded to tell me in an authoritative, scolding tone that I should be putting butter on those burns. However, I knew I was right and I was sticking to my guns.

I told Pete to stand up so I could get a better look at the damage. By this time, those small blisters had joined together and became two giant sacks of water hanging down from his crotch to his knees. We were horrified!

What probably happened was somehow his pants caught on fire. The fabric acted as a wick so it just burned but didn't burn up. Then, he somehow put the flames out not realizing that the skin on his legs had gotten burned so badly. It was a miracle his private parts weren't burned also. At least I don't think so. Just then, my nose reminded me that dinner had been done for quite a while.

I told Pete to just stay in the tub for a little longer. I assured him that everything would be OK—another lie. I was trying to hold my own with Catherine who was still nagging me to get the butter. Also, I was trying to get Dick and Bob another beer. I didn't know it at the time, but I think I was multitasking before it became popular. I put dinner on the table and we all sat down. "Pass the peas please, pass the ketchup please", but after a few moments, I excused myself to check on Pete. You won't believe what I found? While I was doing my hostess thing, Catherine had snuck the butter out of the kitchen, dried Pete off, and covered the blisters with butter!!! Can you imagine this situation?

Here's my son, Tom's future mother-in-law, going unabashedly against me in my own home! A subdued argument ensued between the two of us. Bob and Dick didn't dare utter a word. I have no recollection of any dinner conversation. I was furious at Catherine and didn't know what to say. The damage was done.

There was no way I could get the butter off these two monstrous blisters. I just had to let nature take its course. After the company left, I helped Pete to bed. When he walked, the two sacks of water just sloshed around. I put him to bed with a plastic sheet and a couple bath towels so when they broke it would not soak the bed.

The Heathfield's and I became dear friends over the years, but I still remember Catherine trying to take over my responsibility and good judgment regarding my own family. I think the title of this story is appropriate, it states my situation just as it was—a slow burn!

Motherhood

I know where you go when you die. Well, I know where mothers go, anyway. I can't speak for fathers or men or women in general, but I know about mothers. You go to the pearly gates and when St. Peter comes to you, you hold out your heart and he takes a look. He usually sees bruises, cuts, stitches, and occasionally it's been broken and is still bleeding. Sometimes it's really beat up and even if you've done some really bad things in your life, he just says, "You've paid your dues, go on in."

One thing I don't like about motherhood is that you never know if you are doing it right or not. You never had a chance to practice, and you don't get any results until years later. I never felt confident about how I was raising my kids, especially Barney, my sixth child. He was born on Christmas Eve. He was my Christmas present that year.

Part of the problem was that he was so smart. He was always about ten steps ahead of me. Back in the day, people use to throw really good things out in the trash. There weren't resale shops like there are today. Barney had the most discerning eye. He could discern treasure from trash even when he was young.

One time, a neighbor called and stated she was going to get rid of a really nice wooden salad bowl set. It had eight small matching bowls, a wooden fork, and a spoon that went with the set. She wondered if I wanted it. She said if she put it by the curb, Barney would be there early before the trash man, and would take it home anyway. Barney heard the conversation and ran right down to her house and proudly brought it home.

Once, he built a tree house in our backyard. It was very elaborate. It had rooms and even had carpeting. The only problem was that it was about two feet from a power line. My neighbor, Mrs. Cassidy, called me up and asked if "I knew where Barney was." I said, "Up in the tree house, I guess." When you have lots of kids, it's hard to know specifically where everyone is at any given moment. She chided me properly.

Another time he got the push lawnmower, took it down the street and mowed the grass on the end lot so they could have a place to play. The only problem this time was the field belonged to an old farmer who still lived on the corner. I remember another time when he decided to build a bedroom in our attic. Two problems, you couldn't stand up straight because the roof was too low, and you needed to use a ladder to get up there. I told you we had hard times in those days. These are only a few examples. I could cite dozens more but I'm saving paper. I used to feel so guilty though. It seemed I was always yelling or telling him "no" or "don't do that" about something or other.

My sister and her husband, who live in New York with their five children, suggested I let Barney come and live with them. He was around eight years old. They ran a tight ship with lots of rules and regulations that would be good for him. Knowing I was a single mother, they also thought this would take some strain off me. I was sure they would do a better job and Barney deserved a better life. I had about made up my mind. I was deciding how to tell him that I was sending him away for his own good and that someday he would thank me. We were in the kitchen together. I remember I was doing the dishes and he was eating a cookie. I casually broached the subject telling him of Aunt Joan and Uncle Ed's proposal. I was waiting for his reaction. He got this sly smile on his face and a twinkle in his eye. He glanced at me sideways and said, "You would never send me away, you would miss me too much."

Every once in a while you get immediate feedback on how you are doing and it turns out that you are not doing too badly after all. That's a real gift. Needless to say, the deal was off. My kids and I, we are sticking together no matter what.

St. Vincent de Paul's Angels

Are you ready to hear about another miracle? I've told you we had a lot of them back in those days, but first, let me give you a little background on the situation. My younger brother, Jack, married a girl named Dee, one of six daughters from a devout Catholic family of four young adults and two pre-teens. Several years into the marriage, Dee's father developed cancer and passed away after a long illness. He was only 60 years old when he died. By this time, all five girls were married and the last one had joined the Immaculate Heart of Mary religious order. She became a Nun. This left Mrs. Rourke alone in her Birmingham home, much too big for one person.

Children and grandchildren came to visit often, but it was a lonely life. She decided to sell the big family home and move into a condo in Bloomfield Hills. In the interim, Jack and Dee bought a house in St. Hugo of the Hills Parish and settled in with their six boys. Funny, Dee came from a family of six girls and she had six boys of her own. My brother, Jack, went and still goes to mass every day. He often serves as an altar boy for the Priest when the assigned altar boy is not present. Mrs. Rourke also attended mass daily. Everyone was singing, *Kumbaya* and reading *Kahlil Gibran,* in those days, and *Vatican* two was underway. People wanted to get closer together and become more aware of their fellow man. At this time, Priests began saying mass facing the congregation for the first time in history. Parishioners began greeting each other with, *Peace be with you.* Women were even allowed to pass out the Holy Communion. The church was on fire with zeal to become ecumenical. They always called themselves ecumenical, now they wanted to live it.

Jack and Dee, and Dee's mother Irene developed a close relationship with their Pastor, Father Esper. Mrs. Rourke would come and plant flowers around the rectory and keep fresh flowers on the altar. When a funeral was held at the church, she would arrange to have the catering set up in the social hall afterwards. Finally, Father Esper suggested she take the position as full-time housekeeper. She did not do any cooking or cleaning but worked as an overseer and housekeeper for those positions. She was a lovely and gracious woman and this was the place for her. Also, the position provided living quarters in a small addition to the rectory. It was a cozy place with a beautifully-furnished sitting room, a kitchen and one-small bedroom with connecting bath—perfect for her. The position was supported by a stipend from the St. Vincent DePaul Society. She was given one hundred dollars a month. Mr. Rourke had left his wife very comfortable for life. She never accepted the money. Of course, she knew about our plight. We were all family of sorts. I was occasionally her guest at Oakland Hills Country Club for Sunday Brunch with her family. At the time, I was working as a lunch aide at Baldwin Elementary School uptown. I also had other odd jobs. I used to cut hair and give home permanents to the neighbors (home perms were big back then). I also did some babysitting. Once I sat for Bill Freehan's Gramma and gave her a perm. Remember, he was a star baseball player for the Detroit Tigers? Bill's mother lived in our neighborhood and we were Brownie Girl Scout Troop mothers together.

Anyway, Mrs. Rourke arranged for the money to go to us—one hundred dollars a month—the kids were so excited. We were rich! We accepted this generous gift for a year, and then I felt we were more fortunate than many others. We still lived in our wonderful home in the suburbs. My kids were in good schools that were in walking distance from our home.

Later, when we went on A.D.C. (Aid to Dependent Children); they wanted to move us to a less expensive home, but they couldn't find a place for eight of us and they didn't want to split up the family, so we stayed in the suburbs. See what I mean about *A Charmed Life*?

We explained our feelings and the decision we made. We called Mrs. Rourke and asked if we could come for a visit. I got my sweet children all dressed up. They looked so cute, but they were already cute. We got in our old '55 Studebaker. All eight of us in a six-passenger car and we drove out to Bloomfield Hills. She greeted us at the door with a smile and greeted the kids with a smile and offered the kids a drink. The kids sat quietly and stiffly on her nice furniture. We explained our feelings and the decision we had made and thanked her sincerely for her generosity. A few weeks later, three gentlemen showed up at our door. They were from the St. Vincent DePaul Society; she had given them our name. They came religiously at least once a month and sometimes every two weeks to help. These men lived in our Parish. They all had families of their own, but still took time to reach out to help others. These men were saints who helped save our lives. They came to give support and a lifeline of hope. If I was desperate, I knew I could call anyone of them. They were so much fun and always friendly and interested in the kids' lives. I wanted to recognize them publicly and thank them again for saving our lives. Thank you, Howard Barch, Howard Gagnon, and Frank Schmidt. You are saints. You came to perform miracles for us. Years later, I saw Frank Schmidt in the church parking lot and told him that I had finished MSU and was teaching Special Education. He was surprised and said, "Even with the help, we really didn't think you would make it!" I was stunned at that comment. I still see him occasionally at the library and around town. He always inquires about each of the kids and refers to them by their first names. He commented how he uses us as an example to new clients. He tells them, "If we survived, they could." When you have *A Charmed Life*, it is abound with angels.

A Charmed Life

As I mentioned, I went to college later in life. I think I started at Oakland Community College when I was about 39. There were only three other older women attending that I saw. The trend was just beginning. Remember, this was around the middle of the twentieth century. Things were different then, we were still feeling the shock waves of the 60's hippie generation. Everything was changing.

One of my classmates was trying to sell me a policy for cryonics. That was a process whereby a person who died could be frozen so when a cure for whatever caused their death was found, they could be thawed out and treated for whatever health concern they had. Then, you would carry on with your life. They didn't mention how long the cure might take. Plus, probably all the people you knew, family and friends, would not be around. However, these were modern times, anything was possible. Another popular idea was population "0." Some forecasters predicted the earth was overcrowded and soon we would run out of natural resources, water, land, etc.

One day while walking through the commons area, there was a large gathering of people. Spurred on by my insatiable curiosity, I pushed up to the table to see what was going on. They were asking people to sign a petition to support the idea of over population control. They were going to send it to a Congressman and hopefully get it on the ballot. I have no idea how they could do that, but it was the sixties and anything was possible then. They handed me a pen and pushed the paper in front of me and one zealot said to me, "Do you have any children?" I said "yes" and then they asked me "how many"? I think I almost whispered "seven."

Historically, seven has always been regarded as a lucky number; it surely was my lucky number. The group fell silent.

There was a hush. People began to stare and move away from me until I was alone in the center of this big circle. I should have pulled my shirt up over my head and run for my life, but the crowd just opened up silently and without looking back, I passed safely through and went on to my next class. This was a reconfirmation to me that I never quite fit in the world. But at least they didn't tar and feather me. Like I said, "I've had *A Charmed Life*."

My son, Jack started O.C.C. shortly after I did and one semester we were in the same class together. I believe it was some social-science class. I still remember the teacher's name, it was Mrs. McGregor—you know like in the *Peter Rabbit* tale! We drove out there together in the car but before we went in, Jack gave me the Modus Operandi. "Don't let on that you know me, sit on the other side of the room, and don't even look my way. Got it"?

Not many adults were attending college in those days. I think I saw maybe two other women when I was there and all three of us were mothers.

Well, one of our assignments had to do with genetics. We were to canvas our families and check out whether the subjects had connected ear lobes or detached ear lobes. The other part of this assignment was to also check out whether they could fold/roll their tongues. Of course, my kids were the guinea pigs; they thought it was great fun, sticking out their tongues at each other and pulling each other's ears. These are valid genetic traits. I'm not making this up! Counting me, there were eight of us in this study, a reasonable number of participants to give the findings validity, don't you think? Anyway, I collected the data, charted male and female results regarding these two individualities, and put my homework away.

The next day we handed in our results. After looking the work over, Mrs. McGregor called me up to her desk—I was petrified. She said, "You don't really have seven children do you? Did you falsify the results and contaminate this study?" I think I looked younger than my years due to my size. I was taken aback at her accusation and I swore on my grandmother's grave (my mother was still living, so I couldn't really swear on her grave). Remember, I was right out of the kitchen, a homemaker; what did I know about the hallowed halls of higher learning? I was totally intimidated by the whole place and everyone in it; she cast me a sly smile and with a sideways glance conveyed her skepticism. Then she said, "There's another student in this class with the same last name as you, do you know him?" I broke the trust and confessed that I did, but under no circumstances was I to acknowledge him in public, that was our agreement. We would meet casually at the car to ride home but that was it. We both passed the class but we were never classmates again. I think Jack saw to that.

My First Real Job & Community College

My first job was in the Birmingham Public School as a lunch aide at Baldwin Elementary School in uptown Birmingham. I knew the Director of Special Education, Mr. "M" (remember he was the one who, in a gentle and caring manner, informed me of Pete's intellectual capabilities?). At one of our parent meetings, we were informed that they would be opening a classroom for students who were more educationally challenged than our current special needs students. There were people in the district who scoffed at the idea that Birmingham doesn't have any children who fit that description. Well, of course, they came out of the woodwork; we had more than enough children to fill a classroom.

They had already hired a teacher and Mr. "M" knew my situation, and asked me if I would be interested in a paraprofessional position. I had absolutely no training or education in that or any other area. I only had a high-school diploma and that was many years ago. I admit, I didn't know much, but I did know children. Remember, when I got married, the assumption was that you would not need a job because your husband would take care of you (Are you laughing as hard as I am when you read this?). I had friends who went to college but never worked. They had a husband, they had a husband!

However, this was the sixties and the world was already beginning to turn up-side down. I needed a job and the proximity to home and hours of this position would work out perfectly with my children's schedule. See how *A Charmed Life* always comes into play?

It turned out that I was quite adept at this job in many more ways than I thought. I was good at designing bulletin boards and developing art projects. Of course, I was good at reading stories and acting out rhymes, etc. Those were all things you do with your own children.

After a couple of years at this job, the teacher I worked with suggested I go to college. *What?* I barely got through high school and I had seven children at home. Somehow or another, the idea took hold and I decided to enroll in Oakland Community College, which wasn't too far from my home. Believe it or not, my parents took me out there to register and sign up for my first class. I felt like a little kid on their first day of school. I didn't know what to expect since I was the first in my family to seek higher education. It was very daunting and intimidating for me. Oakland Community College was just being established and the classes were held in trailers or pre-fab buildings. The whole campus was set up on a grassy area probably about three square blocks, maybe four. That was our campus in 1969.

My New Life

Before I graduated from Oakland Community College, I decided to see a counselor since I wasn't sure what to do, or where to go next. I saw Mr. Don Nichols, another lucky encounter for me.

He suggested I go to Michigan State University and get a four-year degree. I was stunned, I said, "We don't have any money." He said, "Go on A.D.C!" His tone was so matter of fact, like *"Elementary, Dear Watson."* I knew what the letters stood for, "Aid to Dependent Children", but we were middle-class-white folk. Incidentally, do you even remember the middle class? A.D.C., how humiliating, demeaning and shameful—ad nauseam! I wasn't even sure how to go about getting on the "dole." I mentioned this possibility to my aunt while I was giving her annual haircut and home permanent.

She was very supportive and encouraged me that those types of programs were for people who were temporarily in need of help. That took some of the sting and shame out of the possibility when thinking about it. So, I got the number out of the phone book and called for an appointment. I was told, "No appointment necessary, just come on in."

Thank heavens for my Dad, he was always there for us, never judgmental or making recriminating remarks, just totally available. He took me out to Pontiac to the Social Services office. I don't exactly remember where it was, I think in the basement of a building, or maybe in an old house.

I went up to the desk and gave my name and informed the clerk why I was there. She gave me a clipboard with a number of papers attached and told me to fill them out and return to her.

I swear it was just like something you'd see in the movies. The room was crowded with women and children (I was the only white woman there). The kids looked poor and sort of unkempt, some of the babies were crying and the little kids were fussy and bored. You could tell most of them had been there for a while. The girl at the desk was doing her nails and had a nonchalant look on her face and an attitude to match.

The room was full and I had no idea how long I would have to wait. I filled out my papers then took them back up to the desk. I asked how long before we would be able see a social worker. "No idea, just sit and wait your turn, here's your number." This whole scenario boiled my white-middle class blood. It was a small glimpse of how hard it is to be poor in America. It was like a chapter from the novel, *The Help*—the timeframe fit.

Finally, I got my turn. "Mrs. Trainor." The worker asked to see my divorce papers. DIVORCED! What? I wasn't divorced! Remember, I was Catholic. We don't get divorced (I was still wearing my wedding and engagement rings). She said, "Well you can't get public assistance unless you're legally divorced!" Hello, World!! I came out and told my Dad. I was totally embarrassed and disheartened. We decided to find the legal offices and get the divorce papers as long as we were out there.

I got the papers, took them home, filled them out, and mailed them right back. I later got a notice stipulating the date, time, and court room in which to appear. I went by myself. I thought it was time for me to grow up and take care of my own business.

Actually, we hadn't seen "Dad" in a while, even when we heard he was around, he seldom called us; and of course, he never sent money. I went to the court on the designated day and when they called my name, I went up through the swinging gate and sat in the witness chair. I was asked, "State your full name." "Dolores Ann Trainor", I replied. The Judge was at his desk next to me but about three feet higher. The clerk then called Dad's name, "Mr. John Trainor." No one answered, so he repeated the name, still no answer.

I was so scared I didn't know what to do or what to say. The Judge asked me where my husband was and whether he sent money. I said, "I don't know and no." Down went the gavel, "Divorce granted, step down!" My new life began.

Queen of Hearts

Remember when the personal growth movement was underway? Everybody was getting into their feelings and doing lots of self-exploration. There were self-help books on every shelf and clients were lined up at the therapist's office (this was before Dr. Phil).

I got caught up in the trend. I had given up homemaking not too long before and was fascinated with the whole idea. I became involved in Transcendental Meditation, took a class in Silva Mind Control, (imagine a name like that?), and got involved in sensitivity training or T Groups as they were called then.

Dr. Symington came up with a method that used visual imagery to cure cancer. You would actually visualize your white blood cells fighting off the invading malignant tumors. I still believe there's a strong case for the mind/body connection. We seem to be learning more and more about this phenomenon—if it can be called that.

Anyway, one time I was having lower back pain. Very unusual for me! I tried to recall whether I'd done any heavy lifting or overdid it at the gym. It hung on for over a week so I decided to take a look at the pain, and see if I could figure out what was so painful "back there."

I had a small couch on a small back porch where I did my meditating. I got comfortable in the seat, rested my hands on my thighs, palms up and open to receiving. I sat quietly, closed my eyes and began to look inward, bringing my attention to the painful area. Oh, what a wonderful sight! I saw myself as a tall, stately Queen. The bodice of my gown was covered lavishly with jewels, mostly with pearls and diamonds. The skirt had a modified hoop covered with layers and layers of gossamer silk and an edge of intricate lace trailing along the hem.

Over my shoulders was draped a full-length white ermine cape with those little black and white tails hanging from the wide-collar-like-tassels. A gold crown had been placed on my head. It had a huge ruby in the center encircled by seven large diamonds. It must have weighed over ten-and-a-half pounds but I didn't seem to mind. I looked relaxed and had a serene smile on my face. I even had a gold scepter in my left hand.

Just then, my skirt sort of opened and all my darling children ran out from underneath!! Running off in every direction!! In an instant, my beautiful dress collapsed down in a big pouf. I felt a burning sensation at the back of my nose and I burst into tears. Fire hot tears! I thought they would scald my cheeks as they flowed down my face. I felt as though my heart was breaking. I cried inconsolably for I don't even know how long and my chest heaving with deep sobs. What happened?

Ever since I was a little girl, I had always wanted lots of children. I had my family in the fifties when motherhood was revered. I never had much self-esteem, but having a big family gave me identity and status in this culture, especially being Catholic. I wasn't one of those Moms who cried when her first-born went off to kindergarten, and I don't remember being particularly sad as each one moved on. I don't remember feeling particularly glad or sad. It just seemed like the natural course of events.

But I must say the happiest time of my life was being a stay-at-home Mom when my kids were growing up. Sweet babies, first teeth, first haircuts, bath times, building forts in the woods, picnics, of course, the list goes on and on—till they leave the nest.

I've had a wonderful full life now, but I guess I never really grieved the loss of those precious years. I thought that was then and this is now and I have to get on with self-actualizing. That was another reward for delving into the murky psyche. It seems I can forget a lot, but my heart remembers and demands its due. I must mourn the loss of wonderful times.

As I became aware through my sobs of the realization of what happened, I bent down and gently picked the dress up and carried it over my arms. I went down some stone steps into a deep cave. It wasn't too big, maybe 9 x 10 feet. It was dimly lit except for a heavenly light shining down in the center. It shone on a golden chair setting up on a low pedestal. I approached the throne and reverently draped the gown over the seat and one arm of the chair.

As I turned to leave, I noticed high-brass gates around the area—the kind you see in a cloister. I silently turned, closed the gate and left. I didn't lock it though. I'll know I can revisit this place in my heart whenever I want. I have since placed other sweet memories there. It's my secret place, or I guess you could say it's my sacred place.

Leaving the little porch, incidentally, where the kids use to play, I wiped the last tears from my swollen eyes. The back pain is gone and I feel very relaxed and peaceful.

The Case of the Infamous Wedding Gown

That title sounds like a *Sherlock Holmes* mystery, doesn't it? Well I guess it is. It all started in 1947. I had just gotten engaged to be married and was setting out to find the picture-perfect wedding dress. Remember, in those days a wedding was a romantic once-in-a-lifetime event? Every bride wanted to look like a virgin princess. Dresses were always white or ivory, bridesmaids wore pastel colors, never black or brown, and never off the shoulder. Also, there were lots of crinoline petticoats under the skirt. Anyway, it was a big deal.

There was a small shop on McNichols, or as we used to call it, Six-Mile Road. It was a few blocks from my old high school, Immaculata, an all-girls high school, where I graduated from a couple of years earlier. The proprietor of the shop, Sophia made all the dresses herself. As I sat and looked at dress after dress, she brought one out and said, "This one is special." It was love at first sight. I had never seen a gown so beautiful—it was an original.

It was a heavy candlelight satin. It had a five-inch wide piece of gathered lace that went down in the front, scooped up over the shoulders, then low in back. The whole area was covered with a fine mesh. It was all but invisible. But modesty and proprietary were everything. And of course, this was topped off with a string of pearls. The long sleeves came to a point over the hands and had satin covered buttons up to the elbows. It was an unusual design. The bodice was fitted and came a little below the waist. Over each hip was a lace covered peplum, it had a Spanish flair.

If I had a fan and a rose, I would have looked like Carmen, the main character in *Bizet's* opera. The train followed behind for about seven feet. It was exquisite and the price was only $300—that was in 1947. Then I came to my senses. *What, $300.00?* Can you imagine how much $300.00 was in 1947? You know how women can rationalize away a minor detail like money when they need to, especially when it comes to buying clothes, especially their wedding dress?

I still needed a little support so I decided to ask my sister-in-law, Irva to come with me and help me make the decision. Irva, my brother Dick's wife, was more comfortable with extravagant purchases than I was. Did I subconsciously choose her to help me? No, I don't think so! When she saw the dress, she immediately fell in love with it also and said, "Dolores, you're only going to get married once, get it!" Do you like this 1940's thinking? Thank you, Irva!

The rationalization went something like this. I had a job; I had my own money; I lived at home I didn't have any bills (this was before charge cards), and I didn't have any responsibilities. Besides, I was going to get married so I would have a husband to take care of me (again, 1940's thinking). I bought the dream dress.

My Mom made me a beautiful braided satin headpiece with little seed pearls clustered on each side. The attached veil floated down to just below my fingertips. After the whirlwind of festivities and showers, the rehearsal dinner, and the wedding breakfast at the Red Run Golf Club, the big day arrived. We were married at Gesu Church, the Parish where I had attended eight years of elementary school, made my first communion, and was confirmed. These milestones were topped off with a honeymoon at Mackinaw Island.

Settling in back at home, I had the precious dress cleaned and stored in an airtight box to seal in all the memories. Then up to the attic for posterity. Every once in a while the kids would take it out and look it over and joke about the old-fashion style. They had seen pictures of me wearing it in photos but that was like ancient history. I don't think kids can imagine their mother as a bride. Besides, they had mostly seen me when I was pregnant, that is a long way from being a bride.

Sharon was the first one of my daughters to get married. She was marrying Dave, her boyfriend of about two years. When we started talking about the wedding, Sharon asked me if I had my old wedding dress. I said, "Of course." I was surprised she was interested. They were both working and paying for their own wedding, so wearing my dress would have been a savings and there was sentimental value. Sharon looked beautiful.

She has brown naturally curly hair, plump cheeks, (we use to call her bubbles when she was a baby). Her hazel eyes and freckles completed the cuteness. Also, she has a contagious laugh and a sweet smile. She's only a few inches taller than I was, so she wore flat shoes. The dress fit her to a "*T*." She was a picture to behold; how sweet, my daughter wearing my wedding dress.

A couple years after that special event, Joan my youngest child, met the love of her life, Michael Jack. Soon they were talking about wedding bells. They were also paying for their own wedding. It's a good thing they were frugal because right after the wedding, they both were laid off from their jobs. Joan starting flipping pizza at Little Caesars and Mike got a job as a dishwasher at Mavericks, a local restaurant. While making plans for the wedding, Joan said to me, "Mom do you still have your old wedding dress?" I said, "Of course."

Back up to the attic to retrieve the special box with the treasured heirloom inside. You should have seen Joan in that gown. She has dark brown hair that flows in soft curls down her back about eight inches below her waist.

How special, two of my daughters wearing their mother's wedding dress.

Lo and behold, a couple of years after that wedding, Carol, who had been living and working in London, England, met the dashing Mark Clewley—a true Brit! They met at a Rugby game. He was on the team and she was in the cheering section. Soon, another wedding date was in the offing and then came the old refrain. "Mom, do you still have your old wedding dress?" I said, "Of course." Back up to the attic.

This was quite a formal affair. The waters of the Atlantic Ocean from the UK to the USA were churning with traveling guests. The groom's mother wore a large hat and carried a big purse. She was a dead ringer for Margaret Thatcher! The gentleman wore morning suits and ascots at their throats. Carol, with her short-dark hair and diminutive figure in this elegant satin gown with the train draped over the steps of the altar, was a picture of propriety.

As they drove off in a stretch limo, amid a rain of rice, both appeared out of the skylights waving to all the happy revelers. With nostalgia, I thought, I really got my money's worth out of that dress.

However, now I'm sorry to tell you the story takes a morbid turn. All the happy memories associated with the enchanted wedding dress slowly began to evaporate. My husband left me after twelve years of marriage and later I got a divorce.

After two children and fifteen years of marriage, Sharon and Dave split up. Mike Jack was killed in an automobile accident after only four years with Joan—he never saw his son. Darling Mark Clewley passed away in 2002 from pancreatic cancer, leaving Carol and their son Tait alone.

We use to think that some of the grandchildren might want to wear the wedding dress, but now we believe it is cursed. We don't know what to do with it. We thought of giving it to a charity, but that seemed risky as some unsuspecting bride might fall in love with it like we did, and who knows what might happen. Hence the title, *The case of the Infamous Wedding Gown*. It's old enough; maybe some museum would like to display it!

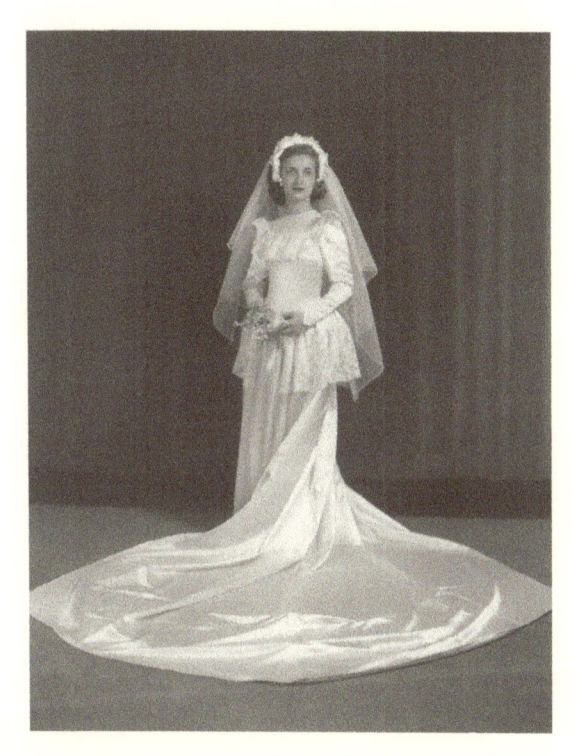

Dee Trainor

60   *A Charmed Life*

Carol Clewley

Sharon & Dave Schmidt, Gramma & Grampa Smith

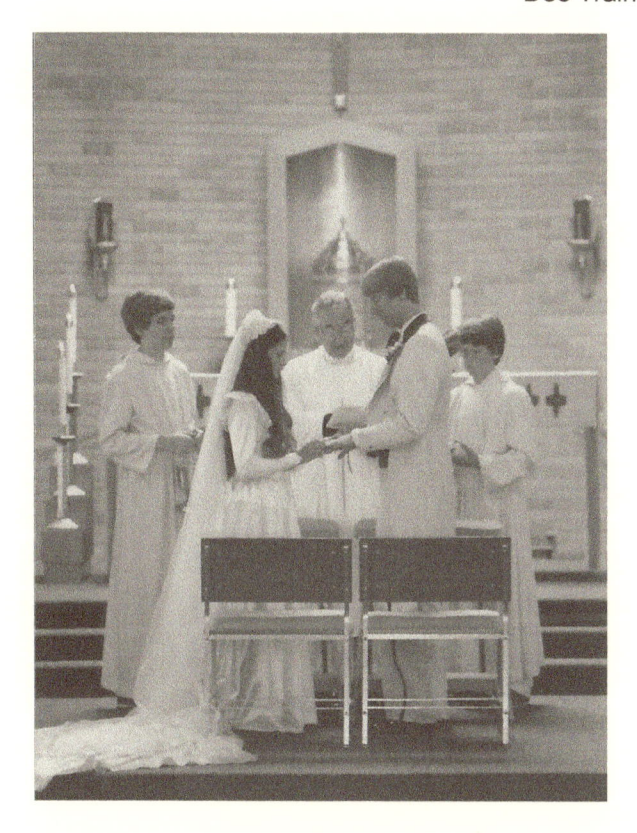

Joan & Michael Jack

Joan and Mike's Wedding

I couldn't believe Joan, my youngest child was going to get married and leave home. It seemed uneventful when the other kids left; sometimes moving in and out a couple of times before leaving for good. However, this was the end. Joan always said she was born in this house and was not going to move out until she got married. She stuck to her word.

I remembered back to my wedding day almost 36 years ago to the day, July 17, 1948. The temperature was the customary 80 plus degrees. No air conditioning at Gesu, my church back then, and now at Our Lady Queen of Martyrs—it was hot.

I proudly walked Joan down the aisle. She said I was her Mom and Dad all those years and she wanted me to give her away. All eyes were on this sweet radiant bride wearing her mother's wedding dress; her wavy hair cascading down her back and the long satin train following behind.

We met Mike at the altar rail. He was about 6'3" and Joan was 5'5". She took his arm and together they ascended the steps up to the kneelers in front of the altar. The bridesmaids and groomsmen flanked both sides of the platform.

I turned and took my place in the second row next to my parents. Behind me was the rest of the family, Jack, Barney, Tom, Patty, Pete and so on down the line. Father Villeroit greeted the couple, turned and mass began. Epistle, Gospel, stand up, sit down, sing a hymn, stand up and sit down again, softly recite a few *"Lord have Mercies"*, etc. Tom, my second son, gave the reading. It was a quote from *Kahlil Gibran* (remember this was in the eighties). It was something about your children not being your children, they are like arrows that we only have for a short time, and then we send them out into the world.

I was crying and wiping my eyes and crying and wiping my nose and crying. Now came the long awaited moment, the wedding. Joan and Mike each walked around their kneelers and stood in front of the Priest. Father Villeroit began talking about the importance of this sacred union. The devotion of husband and wife to each other, he stressed the Christian role of each.

Slowly Joan begins to lean her head over on Mike's shoulder. It was such a touching scene it brought more tears to my eyes and I thought, isn't that sweet, I need more tissues. Then, Joan began to slowly lean more and more on Mike. He seemed oblivious. He was staring straight ahead and continued to pay attention to what the Priest was saying. I then realized that Joan was slowly melting down. I turned slightly to Jack behind me and whispered out of the corner of my mouth, "Do something, go up there." Then, from the back of the church, my nephew, who happened to be in med school at the time, walked up the aisle, and as he passed me, I got up and followed him. We climbed the altar steps and just as Joan was beginning to crumble, we grabbed her under each arm. I was thinking; do not slip on the long satin train.

We whisked her away from the groom (he never looked at us) went down the steps as we crossed in front of the gathered guests and headed out the side door. We sat her on the walk and leaned her up against the granite wall. The custodian brought over orange juice per the "doctor's" orders. After a few minutes, Joan began to come around.

This must have been a first because no one seemed to know what to do, so they did nothing. That had not happened at the rehearsal the night before! Joan had probably fainted from the heat. The beautiful wedding dress acted like a plastic bag; and of course, she had not eaten either, so she probably just got dehydrated.

After several minutes, Joan said she felt well enough to go back into the church. We helped her up, swung the long train around so she would not trip, and pushed through the large oak doors. As we reentered the inner sanctum, it felt like a time warp. It was as though nothing had happened. The organist was still playing and the congregation continued to respond to the Priest, *"God have Mercy."* Mike was still standing, albeit alone, in front of Father Villeroit who was still holding the open missile and reading the wedding ceremony. Joan climbed up the steps, walked around the kneelers and took her place next to Mike, who was still standing and looking straight ahead as though nothing had happened. Not to miss a beat, the Priest declared, "And now I pronounce you man and wife. You may kiss the bride."

The whole congregation broke into a thunderous applause and wild cheers. The wedding marched commenced and the happy couple turned to face family and friends with heads held high and beaming smiles, they paraded back down the aisle through the high oak doors and onto the veranda. Everyone was laughing and congratulating the happy couple and throwing the perfunctory rice. Joan always said she was glad she got back to the ceremony in time for the most important part. "What was that Joan?" When the Priest said, "I now pronounce you man and wife."

We Lose Mike

I just came back from a nice brisk walk. It is in the fifties and cloudy. I love the weather when it's like this; it feels so fresh and invigorating. I love to walk. When I go out the front door, I stand there and say to myself, which way should I go? How about through the woods, or over to the church for a visit? Of course, it's always interesting to walk down Southfield Road towards the shops: Target, TJ Maxx, Borders, and the others. You can see how difficult it is to decide! Each way has its own appeal.

I decided to go to the shops on 13 Mile Road. It is just a gravel drive, but I see they have a few small offices along there. The names are connected with the mortuary business. This is no surprise because this road is behind and connected to the cemetery. I've been back there before. You can see old trucks and cement casings that go into the ground to hold the caskets, piles of dirt, old tree stumps, and small earth moving equipment; all sorts of old junk.

As I go over the hill past the new military memorial burial grounds, I can see the beautiful building with its figures and symbols carved into the stone. The Masons built it back in the twenties and when a funeral procession enters the grounds, the bell tower chimes out the most beautiful nostalgic music. I can hear it all the way to my apartment. It's sweet albeit bitter. Coming down the hill, I can see across the path, a grave set between three small trees. It seems as though it was just nestled as planned. It is covered with a Christmas grave blanket. You may have seen them; they're made of balsam tree branches and pine cones tied together with bright red ribbons and bows. It was the first one I've seen this year.

I also know this place because my second oldest son, Tom worked here in the summer while attending Michigan State University. He planted flowers and repainted the high wrought iron fence that surrounds these sacred grounds. Yes, it's the beginning of Christmas Tide and I'm taken back to 1985 to the sights, the sounds, and the scents of that Christmas.

My youngest daughter, Joan and her husband Mike had been married about two-and-a-half years at this time. They were both working now and had just purchased the house where Mike had grown up from his parents. They were having such a good time turning it into their home. Mike commandeered the basement. The first thing to catch your attention as you came down the stairs was the light from the flashing beer sign. His precious memorabilia included Tigers pendants, a football signed by one of the Detroit Lions, and the most revered, the trophy he had won while playing hockey with his Dad and two brothers. This was displayed in a prominent place on a special shelf that Mike had built himself. Joan had her jewelry bench in the back. She had a gas line hooked up for soldering and electrical outlets set up for buffing and polishing stones. She did jewelry repairs for a couple of jewelers in town. Everything was going according to plan and now it was time to start a family. When nature did not comply with the plans, the doctor suggested a simple medical procedure to increase Joan's chances of getting pregnant.

On December 20th, even though she was still recuperating, Joan and Mike planned on going to buy their first Christmas tree to put up in their new house when Mike got home from work. Joan called me around 4:00 and said, "Mike wasn't home yet." She wanted to know if I could go uptown to the Mole Hole to pick up a gift she had purchased the week before. She wasn't driving yet. I said, "Sure, I'll be right over." We shopped around a bit and then Joan began getting tired. We gathered up our packages and left.

We were admiring all the beautiful colored lights adorning the homes and trees as we drove back down Pierce Street. What a beautiful time of the year! I dropped Joan off at her house. Mike's blue truck wasn't in the driveway yet. He probably stopped off for a drink with the boys after work. It was his last day before vacation.

As I pulled into my driveway on Birwood Street, Barney came out the front door and around to the driver's side of my car. He told me to move over and he got into the driver's seat. As he backed out into the street, I asked him, "What's wrong, where are we going?" Looking straight ahead, he said "Joan's." I said, "What for, I just came from there?" He didn't say anything; he just began to drive down Greenfield faster than usual. I turned, facing him and said, "What happened"? No answer. I said anxiously, "There's been an accident?"—half guessing— still no answer from Barney. Passing 13 Mile Road, I cried out in desperation, "Is Mike hurt, is he dead?" His face said it all. I said, "Floor it Barney. Don't stop at that red light ahead (12 Mile Road) keep going, faster!" As we pulled in front of Joan and Mike's house, I saw a police car in the driveway. When Barney and I burst through the front door, the nightmare had already begun.

Joan was lying on her back on the couch with her knees pulled up against her chest. She was rocking and crying. She said, "He can't be dead, he's only hurt, I can take care of him. I don't care how bad it is, I'll take care of him." I fell down on my knees next to the couch. I was holding Joan's hand and trying to console her, I guess. Actually, I have no idea what I said. We were beyond heartsick.

I looked around and saw a policeman talking to my son-in-law, Dave. Dave was a deputy for the Oakland County Sheriff's Department. He took care of all the gory details, like identifying the body, etc. Dave's son, my little grandson Michael was peeking out the half-closed bedroom door. He didn't know what was going on.

My oldest son, Jack arrived and he called my second oldest son, Tom in New Jersey. Later, Tom said when he got the news he felt like someone punched him in the stomach. Then Jack called Carol. My oldest daughter, Carol and her boyfriend, Mark had just returned to England after a week-long pre-Christmas visit with the family. They had spent lots of time with Joan and Mike. Joan was crying and calling out, "Carol, come home."

Carol knew she couldn't come right back. She was crying and so upset. Next, I opened the front door and saw my daughter, Sharon and her friend, Karen. They were just standing there and staring at me in disbelief. Their eyes were as large as saucers. I guess they were waiting for me to tell them that the whole thing was a mistake. They came in and sat on the floor next to Joan. Everyone was walking around in a stupor not knowing what to do.

After a while Jack took over. He told me to take Joan home with Barney and me. He gave me some pills to calm her down and help her sleep. He stressed the importance of the medication, but to only take one tonight and probably one tomorrow. We've never been a family that relies much on medication. I got Joan's Christmas pajamas and put them in a bag. You should have seen them; red and white vertical stripes with feet and a trap door in back. They had white lace around the neck and down the buttoned front. We got her coat and then Barney and I bundled her up and took her home to my place on Birwood. I gave her the pill and tucked her under the covers. I quietly went around to the other side of the bed and slid into bed beside her, weeping silently.

When she woke up the next morning, she looked at me and said, "Mom, was that a dream?" I said, "No." She turned her head away, squeezed her eyes shut and began to sob. Her chest was heaving but she didn't make a sound. After a while we got up. She got dressed and asked me if I would give her a ride home. I said, "Joan, stay here awhile with Barney and me." She said, "If I don't go home now, I will never go back." Mike was only 26 years old.

Joan's Pregnancy

Did I mention that two of my daughters are widows? I'll tell you about Joan first. She's my youngest child. She lost her husband in a terrible automobile accident when she was 23 years old. It was the worst thing that ever happened to our family.

In the winter of 1984, Joan and Mike had purchased their first little home and were ready to start a family. After they were unsuccessful with getting pregnant, Joan discovered that she had a condition called endometriosis. Doctors recommended that she have a medical procedure that hopefully would encourage pregnancy. This happened just a few days before Mike died. The fact that she hadn't gotten pregnant before his death was even more devastating for Joan. She even wondered if they could get some sperm from his body after his death. But that was impossible at that time.

Our Christmas party at my house was a week or so after the funeral. Joan didn't come, nor did she answer the phone. I was so worried. I sent Jack and Tom, her older brothers, to her house to get her. When they got there she was in bed wearing Mike's pajamas. They persuaded her to come home with the family, which she reluctantly did.

As the weeks passed, Joan didn't seem to recover. She lost weight and was sick much of the time. We were so worried; we thought she was just going to pine away. After a month or so, we sent her to New Jersey to visit her brother, Tom and his family. We thought the change would be good for her, but it didn't help. So, when she returned she made an appointment with her doctor.

As she was being examined, the doctor said, "You're pregnant." Joan said, "Who are you talking to?" The doctor said, "You, Joan, you're pregnant!" The nurse said "What, she can't be, she had a D and C procedure?" The doctor said, "Well, she is." Joan was *over the moon* as they say. She said, "Now I have a part of Michael."

For me, it was bittersweet. I was so happy for Joan, but I know how hard and lonely it is to be a single Mom. There were a number of heart-rending situations ahead of us. Many times Joan was singled out and pitied which is definitely not Joan's persona. She never complained or felt sorry for herself. My heart broke many times for her and I had to fight back the tears. Like when we packed up the baby shower gifts and sent Joan home alone to put things away in the nursery. Joan's strength always won the day.

Once, we thought of joining a grieving group. There was one held at a church nearby. Joan and I went in, put our nametags on, and then took a chair in one of the small circles. Each group had a facilitator that directed the conversation. As each person told their story, others nodded with empathy. When it came to Joan, they realized she was a widow. She said she lost her husband in an automobile accident and she was here with her Mom. Since I was with her, and because of my age, they thought I was the widow and my six-month pregnant sweet daughter came to support me. We never went back.

Joan decided to use the Lamaze method for delivering her baby. She needed a partner. Guess who won? Me! It was heartbreaking for me. Four sessions were offered to practice something called the team method. So there we were, Joan lying on a mat on the floor with her big belly, a pillow, and a small stuffed bear with a red bow. The bear was the object she was to stare at to keep focused. I was sitting on the floor alongside of her. I was helping her to remember to control her breathing. When a contraction came, she was to start panting with short quick breaths until the pain subsided. Then, she was to relax until the next one. I learned where to rub her back, stroke her hair and face to comfort her. Of course, we were laughing like we always do. But inside, my heart was breaking for Joan. All of the other young Moms had a loving husband sharing this momentous event.

Finally, the big day arrived on August 15th. Joan called me that morning and said she thought her pains were starting (as usual, I didn't know what to say!). After giving birth to seven children, you would think I'd be an expert, but I wasn't sure what to do. Was it time or not? Soon, I went over to Joan's house and we went to the hospital. I called one of the kids and the fan out of calls went into effect. Shortly after we arrived, the waiting area outside her room was full of people. Soon, we passed the allowed number of guests but still they came, some sneaking in. A few hours in, the contractions began in earnest. Finally, when I was leaning over her face and instructing and demonstrating the panting procedure, Joan reached up and grabbed me around the neck and pulled me into her face and yelled, "Mom I can't take it anymore!" Just then, the doctor said, "That's it Joan, here comes your baby." Joan let go of my head and began to relax. The doctor gave me a pair of scissors and said, "Here Grandma, you can cut the cord." Joan was beaming!

A baby boy, James had the face of an angel. He was the most beautiful baby in the world. There were more heartbreaking reminders as time went on.

When James was to be baptized, Joan was holding him as they stepped to the altar. The Priest called out, "Would the father please come forward." Then, my son-in-law, Dave stepped up and said softly that the father had passed away, and that he would take his place.

Joan has gone on to be James' father and mother: attending parent teacher meetings, father and son dinners, etc. After 25 years, he is not cute anymore, just handsome. To remember how cute James was, I painted a picture of him when he was about ten years old.

James Jack

Painting in Italy
(Keeping the wine safe)

Somehow or other, strange things seem to happen to me. Not bad things, but unusual things; things that don't seem to happen to other people. Like Charlie Brown, I seem to have this small cloud over my head that follows me around wherever I go—not a black cloud mind you, but sort of a gray one.

As an example: Around the year 2000, I went on a trip to Italy with ten other artists. We were going there to paint. Can you imagine? Painting in Italy where all the great masters used to paint. Altogether we were 13. Three husbands came along to chauffer us around. Can you imagine a sacrifice of that magnitude? That must be love.

Upon our arrival, we rented two cars and headed for Gaiole in Chianti nestled in the hills of Tuscany. I felt like Audrey Hepburn, and I'm sure I heard music from *The Pines of Rome* by Respighi wafting over the terra cotta tile roofs of the villages as we climbed the narrow roads. We pulled up to the beautiful villa we had rented. One husband got out and opened the gates. We drove over the cobble stone drive, past the swimming pool, rose covered trellises and colorful gardens. There were small, connected brick suites lining both sides of the courtyard. Each one designed to accommodate two-to-four occupants. They had a kitchen, bathroom, living room, and two bedrooms. I was staying in the main villa in a room with a very low ceiling that nobody wanted. It was perfect for me (I'm about 4'11").

I shared a suite with one of the couples, Dr. Dick and his wife, Eleanor. A small window in my room overlooked the courtyard so I always knew what was going on. I'm like that at home too. I like to keep track of whose going to work or church, shopping or the like. We ate in the open-air kitchen with a fireplace that took up one whole wall. The hearth could accommodate four standing people comfortably. For lunch we picked ripe tomatoes and snipped fresh basil from enormous painted ceramic pots stationed around the courtyard. We then added mozzarella balls, balsamic vinegar, and extra virgin olive oil. We dipped fresh baked Italian bread in the dressing.

Our sightseeing included Rome, Florence, etc. We saw magnificent sculptures, Michelangelo's *David*, the *Pieta*, and paintings in the Vatican. We were in heaven. Back at our villa, we set up the easels and did our plein aire painting right from our courtyard. A couple of times we painted right in the olive groves across the street!

A few days before our departure we went shopping in town, which was only a few miles from where we were staying. Some were buying stoneware service for eight, garlic graters made out of olive wood, aprons with pictures of the coliseum; and of course, we found some great buys at Violeta, the wine tasting festival that was being held in the town square.

At the week's end, we packed everything in the cars: easels, paint, brushes, canvases, and pastels (those were mine). We dumped the turpentine, that won't fly, and then loaded the artists. Finally we checked that the husbands had gas in the cars and the correct directions to the airport. With tears in our eyes, we blew kisses and vowed to return soon, parting with an *arrivederci* or something like that. Then we headed down the narrow winding road back to civilization.

In the airport we all stayed fairly close together and relied on Dick Gause or rather Dr. Gause who seemed to automatically step in as our guide/director. We had plenty of time; we found our gate and just kind of hung around and reminisced about our experience.

One friend, Kathy M. purchased three cartons of wine, four bottles to a carton. I didn't have much to carry because I use a backpack and a hip purse when I travel. I don't have many character flaws; but I do have one, I always want to help everyone. Maybe because I have been a single Mom for years, maybe because I was a Special Ed Teacher, maybe because I always had to help my Mom, whatever the cause, that's the way it is.

Anyway, I offered to carry two of her cartons because she seemed to be struggling with them in addition to her other things. She's younger than I am and strong and healthy. Why was I trying to help her? It was her fault for buying so much wine, even when it was a bargain. She's spoiled! She has a doting husband who does everything for her. Anyway, she let me help her. As I walked along, the bottles were clinking together. Some people were looking at me, but I thought, oh well, they should mind their own business. It was time to line up at the ticket counter. I'm fifth in line and Dr. Dick, the tall good looking gentleman who has a mild manner, but is used to getting what he wants, was standing behind me.

The clerk looked at my ticket and said, "You're not on this flight, your plane is at Gate 21 and is scheduled to take off in five minutes. You better run or you will miss your flight!!!" I started to say, "There must be some mistake", and then Dr. Dick stepped up and said, with a soft voice and a smile, "No, she's with us, were all traveling together." The clerk replied in a slightly higher register, "She's not with your group, her plane is LEAVING! I'll see if they will hold for a minute otherwise she will be stranded right here in Italy." My friends began to mutter questions as the clerked picked up the phone and contacted the plane, MY plane.

Dr. Dick was trying to reassure the others and remind them that there is a layover in Florence. We will meet there and all fly back together. I'm in shock. I take my ticket back, pick up my, *ah her wine*, and start to run in the direction that the attendant pointed. I had to sort of squat down a bit to keep the wine bottles on an even keel so they wouldn't crash together and make so much noise, or God forbid, break and spill all over the floor. Remember how Groucho Marx used to kind of run low? That was me!

I don't know how I even found the gate. I don't speak Italian nor do I read it! The best I could do, other than Pig Latin, was *Polly voi Franca* and I knew that wouldn't help. Or, maybe I should have said *arrivederci*, but I didn't know what that meant either. I was shaking when I breathlessly arrived at the plane. They were expecting me and anxious to depart. I climbed up the few metal steps and the stewardess took my hand, pulled me in and closed the door. She quickly put me in the jump seat right next to the cockpit and clicked my seat belt. Within seconds the plane pulled away from the ground and off into the wild blue yonder. My first thought, of course—was is the wine safe? Of course, I'm trustworthy. I had incautiously set it down between my feet. *Thank you, Jesus!* I wanted to cry. I could hardly hold back the tears. The hostess sat across from me and just stared.

As we ascended, she said something to me in Italian but I said, "I don't speak Italian." She seemed perturbed. Maybe I had her seat? Anyway, she said in accented English that after the seat belt sign went off, she would find me a seat back with the other passengers.

I arrived at Metro a few hours ahead of the others because of their layover in Florence. I was lucky as I got to fly straight through, ALONE! Should I wait for them? Hell no! I was really angry by that time. I wanted to know who got the tickets. Which travel agency made such a stupid mistake? I was furious. No, I'm not waiting for those guys. All traveling together, safe, comfortable, and having fun. The hell with them, I got my luggage, hailed a cab while still keeping the wine safe. I headed for home still feeling sorry for myself, why me?

After my shower, some of the husbands who were picking their wives up at my apartment began to arrive. Jokingly, I began to relay my sad plight. They were all very sympathetic which made me feel a little better. You know that martyred feeling is sometimes very sweet.

Remember Kathy, whose wine I was nice enough to carry across continents? Her husband met her at the gate with a bouquet of flowers because he missed her so much! I told you she was spoiled. I tried to get some compensation from the travel agency, but of course, that never happened. In case you doubt the validity of the cloud premise mentioned at the beginning of this story, I've documented other unusual situations to substantiate this strange phenomenon. You are probably wondering about Kathy's wine? No, I didn't drink it; although I should have to teach her a lesson.

Karen, another artist who was on the trip, and I decided to meet Kathy at the South Lyon hotel for lunch so I could hand over the coveted contraband. I was glad to be rid of the responsibility. I could just imagine one of my kids coming over when I wasn't home thinking it was a gift for them, opening and downing a bottle.

We really enjoyed ourselves laughing and recounting the adventure. After a nice meal, we parted ways with hugs all around. On the way home, driving east on 696, I said to Karen, "How much do I owe you for lunch?" thinking she had charged the bill to her account. She said, "I didn't pay the bill, I thought you did!" On no, I suggested she call Kathy and ask if she had paid. Well you guessed it; we walked out without paying the tab!! We didn't run, you'd think someone would have seen us and told our waitress. Well, we decided Kathy should go back and settle up, she lived the closest. She went pronto. The manager and waitress were very unhappy with her, but she's spoiled and knows how to defend herself from crises. We had a good laugh over that. Either way, they should have known better than to hang out with me.

Missing Mother Teresa

Believe it or not, my nephew was ordained into the priesthood by *Pope John Paul II*. People don't believe me when I tell them that. It was in 1986, my two brothers, their wives, and I decided to attend this momentous occasion. My sister, her husband, and their six other children were flying to Rome from their home in New Hampshire to witness the ceremony welcoming their brother into the Order of the Oblates of the *Blessed Virgin Mary* of the Holy Roman Catholic Church. Eddie Broom was going to become a Priest.

You can imagine the importance of this event. It's probably the highest honor a catholic family can receive; having one of their children ordained a Priest. We were all thrilled and let the special blessings cascade down over us. We were all humbled and proud.

Well, if you remember in 1986, the world situation was looking pretty bleak. The *Cold War* between the USSR and the USA was beginning to heat up. Russia had been making serious threats against the West and the government was discouraging air travel to Europe. Everyday more and more flights were being cancelled. My two brothers reluctantly cancelled their trip.

At the same time, my niece Julie, an art student was in Italy wresting marble from the mines of Carrere. Her family was concerned about her safety but decided to allow her to stay and finish her studies, which would culminate in about a month.

My son-in-law, Michael had just been killed in an auto accident in December. Now it was March, I don't think I was thinking very clearly so I just went as planned making the trip alone. I flew to England, changed planes in London then flew into Germany. Jackie, the wife of another one of my nephews, Tom Broom met me.

He was a First Lieutenant in the Army. I spent two nights with them. Walking around the town was surreal. I walked past a cemetery. Seeing names on the graves of soldiers and people, who we were at war with when I was younger, was a very strange experience.

For lunch, Jackie and I had a wiener schnitzel and a cold stein of German beer before I left for the train bound for Rome, the Eternal City. When I travel alone, which is most of the time, I try to look around for someone I think I can relate to and then strike up a conversation and hang with them. I found a young girl, a student at a university. We hit it off. She gave me tips on people to stay away from when I told her I was sleeping on the top bunk. She reminded me to keep my valuables—passport and money—tight around my waist under my clothes.

My brother-in-law met me at the train station. We drove to the seminary where the rest of the family was and where we would stay for the few days before the ordination. My nephew, "Father Ed" seemed to be well known everywhere he went. He was a regular "Altar Boy" for the *Pope*. Also, he used to say mass for the nuns and novices at *Mother Teresa's* House in the city. He took us there one day. It was just a tiny place sparsely furnished and no yard. We had to take our shoes off on the porch before we went in; she wasn't there, of course. Probably off to India or some other exotic place. However, we got to meet and talk with her little sister and novices anyway. They were all giggling and scurrying around doing their chores. They were so sweet and friendly and so glad to see us, especially Father Ed.

After a short visit, Father Ed blessed us, said a few prayers and we were on our way. What a thrill, *Mother Teresa's* house!

Walking up the aisle of St. Peter's Basilica was like a dream. Everything was just like I had seen in books and movies but much larger than I ever could have imagined. I was sitting next to my niece, Julie. We were in the fifth row and the second seat in when the Pope walked by sprinkling Holy Water on the congregation. I could have reached out and touched him. This was a once-in-a-lifetime experience. After the ceremony, we retired to the monastery for the evening, totally exhausted but exhilarated. What a day!!

The next day my niece had to go into Rome to change her airline ticket. I offered to go along for company. We took a train to town. We made a couple of false starts, but finally found the airline office on the first floor of a building. At the front door, we had to press a button to gain entry. We could see clerks looking out the window at us. We could also see several soldiers wearing green berets, holding AK47's along with Doberman Pincers on chain link leashes. This was a new experience for us, two small town girls from America's suburbs. We'd never seen anything like this except in the movies.

They let us in and searched our purses and any bags we were carrying. We answered their questions then proceeded to the counter and Julie spoke to the clerk through a small opening in the two-inch thick glass. With the new ticket in hand, we left looking at each other, we said, "Wow that was exciting."

As we walked around the street, we noticed there weren't many people out. We thought, well, it wasn't crowded; we might as well have lunch and shop a bit. Never mind that there were soldiers looking out some windows in the buildings with guns! Julie was only in her twenties, but I should have known better. We were just taking in the sights enjoying ourselves. Finally, we decided we had better get back. When you stay at a monastery, they expect you go by their rules and regulations. Breakfast was at seven, lunch at 12:30, etc. You can't just decide you want a snack in the middle of the day. No potato chips or pop! On our way home, Julie and I realized how late we were. We were laughing and joking about their rules. We sounded like two rebellious kids, but underneath we were also scared a bit. We thought they would probably be angry with us.

Taking a shortcut home from the train station, we went through an alley. All these junkyard dogs were barking at us and threatening to tear us to shreds. I was terrified. We walked faster and faster. As we walked, we began to manufacture excuses for our tardiness. Definitely not our fault! We were victims of circumstances. "Let's keep our stories straight. Don't mention that we had gone shopping and out for lunch. We'll ditch the shopping bags, I said." We braced ourselves and walked into the dining room. No one was there. Not a soul. The room was empty.

We heard voices behind us and slowly turned around. In came the whole family, laughing and talking. They were so excited; they had gone to *Mother Teresa's* house and SHE WAS THERE! They spent about an hour with her joking and laughing. They were telling us all about the visit. They said *Mother Teresa* was wearing a lei around her neck that someone had given her; she took it off and put it around Father Ed's neck. He said, "No, Mother on you" as he put it back around her neck. She removed it and put it back on Father Ed, "No, Father on you." Then she said, "Let me kiss your hands Father, you bring Jesus to us." He said, "No, Mother let me kiss your hands."

Anyway, they were all overwhelmed laughing and retelling the story of their visit. They were thrilled and ecstatic—imagine a chance to meet *Mother Teresa* of Calcutta in person?

After a while, when the excitement began to wind down, my sister looked at me and said, "How was your day Dee?" I said, "Great, (I lied) we got the ticket changed and all went well." "Good", my sister said, "sorry you missed *Mother Teresa* though." Julie and I looked at each other totally disheartened and sad. *Mother Teresa* is one of my favorite people in the world. Well, I guess it wasn't meant to be.

Mother Teresa, Mary (niece) & Mike (nephew)

Mom's Last Day

Marie Smith

My Mom was an amazing woman. She passed away when she was 104 years old. She lived during three centuries. Born in January 1898 and died in March 2002 *St. Patrick's Day*. She also maintained good health overall throughout those years. She had a few instances that were worrisome, but she always seemed to bounce back. Her real cross was that she was hard of hearing (we never said deaf). She underwent surgery as a result of a mastoid behind the ear when she was about twelve years old. Surviving a surgery like that in 1910 was quite remarkable.

My mother was very intelligent, but due to her disability, not always being able to hear someone speak, made life very hard for her. She said she always felt dumb because she wasn't always sure what was going on or how to respond. In her 60's, she was treated for a torn retina. During her mid-seventies, she had colon cancer. They removed the encapsulated tumor. No further treatment. She never had any cancer again. When she was in her early nineties, she broke her hip. The doctors replaced it and she went on her way, many times without a walker.

Another time, she caught the flu and had to be taken to the hospital because she got dehydrated. Each time we all said, "Well, that's the end of her" and each time she recovered. Another example: Once she said she had a terrible pain in her temple and collapsed—off to the hospital again. We thought for sure this was the end. A stroke in your nineties is not good. We all stood around her bed with long, worrisome faces waiting for the worst. She began to stir, opened her eyes and said, "What happened? The last thing I remember was this terrible pain right here", as she touched her temple. We all just looked at each other and declared that she was totally indestructible. She would probably bury us all!

However, near the end of 2001, Mom's mental health began to decline. I noticed a dramatic change when I returned from England after the funeral of my son-in-law. He passed away in December and I had stayed a week or so after to help my daughter with her house and other matters.

It was apparent to the staff that Mom needed more than just assisted living, she needed nursing care. She was moved to the back wing of the nursing home. There's a whole other world back there. However, we weren't concerned because of her history of knocking at death's door and then laughing in his face since, her facility for recovery was legendary.

It was *St. Patrick's Day*, March 17, 2002. My plan was to visit Mom, and then go to Vasu-Lynch Funeral Home to look at pictures, reminisce, and pay respects to the family of a dear friend of mine. I would stay there about an hour and then head to South Lyons to my daughter's house. As I walked down the hall to Mom's room, she was being wheeled towards me on her way to the dining room. I was shocked to see the state she was in. Her white hair, usually neat and brushed, was sticking out in frenzy, no earrings, no lipstick, no colorful scarves at her neck. Where was the coveted purple shawl?

Her eyes were wide open and frantic. She saw me as we approached each other and called out, "Dee, what's happening to me"? She knew something was wrong. The aide continued on, oblivious to the panic in Mom's voice. They put Mom in a chair at a table for eight. Most of the patients had to be fed. You know the scene? Big diapers used for bibs, blank stares, some tied to their chairs to keep them from slumping to the floor, some babbling but with no conversation; and of course, the ever present odor of urine. No Febreeze, Lysol, perfume or incense can ever mask those fumes.

This is not meant to be a condemnation of this wonderful facility. They took very good care of my mother, she was always happy and content there. It is the best way we know to care for our loved ones, when we can't do it ourselves.

Seeing my Mom in that state was totally surreal. Could this be my mother who was always up on things, using the phone, writing in her journal every day? Was this the same person who would call every staff member by name, asking about their families? Chiding me for not coming to visit more often; and when I did, complaining that I was always late. No, this time she is not going to recover.

I pulled up a chair next to her. She was starting to rock back and forth and tilt her chair backwards. She was acting like all the other women in this section, but I knew she wasn't like them. I was trying to feed her. She would have been so humiliated if she realized what was going on. I suppose everyone says the same thing when this happens in their family. She didn't even seem to know what to do with the food in her mouth.

I remembered a story my sister-in-law told me about her mother when she was dying of cancer. She said, "Mom, why don't you give up and let go, you've suffered long enough." Her mother then just peacefully went to sleep and passed on. I always thought what a wonderful thing. Sometimes we just need permission to do something.

Then, I thought that's what I'll do for Mom. But you know enough about her by now to know that telling HER what to do, especially me telling her what to do, was not the script that had played out over our lifetime together. But that was then, this is now. Now I'll decide. I turned to her and said, "Mom" in a loud firm voice, remember she was deaf and she didn't have her hearing aide in. "Mom, when you go back to your room, go to sleep and don't wake up, go with Dad." She feebly looked at me and said, "I'll try." I said again in a loud and firm voice, "No, don't try, you can do it. When you go back to your room, go to sleep and don't wake up. Go with Dad."

She finished eating. I said goodbye and "don't forget what I said." A staff member wheeled her away. As I got to the door to leave the dining room, the head nurse came up to me and said, "I think that was terrible; the things you said to your mother. Also, you've upset the other patients talking like that. Don't you ever do that again or I'll refuse to let you in this section." Well, the patients who were in this section didn't even know who or where they were. They couldn't comprehend what I was saying even if they wanted to.

But then, she didn't know me. She didn't know that I was a frequent visitor and that I always took my mother out to dinner, doctors, dentist appointments, and attended all social functions.

One time when I was taking her to the dentist, we passed the lounge where other clients were sitting. They asked where we were going and I said, "The dentist." They asked me if she was having trouble with her dentures. Mom and I looked at each other with a puzzled look, and I said, "No, she is having her teeth cleaned." She still had her own teeth! This was when she was 103 years old.

I left St. Anne Meads and then spent time at the funeral home looking at pictures and socializing with friends. Then I paid my respects to the family and drove off to South Lyons to spend the night at my daughter Joan's house. As I drove along 696, I answered my cell phone. It was the nurse from the Mead. She said, "Mrs. Trainor?" "Yes", I said. "This is the nurse from the Mead, your mother is not responding." "Oh, (pausing) then I said, "What do you want me to do?" Silence …she hesitated and then said, "I just thought you would want to know." "OK, thanks for calling", I replied.

Shortly after I arrived at Joan's, my phone rang again. We were standing around the kitchen table just chatting at that time. "Hello, Mrs. Trainor?", "Yes", I said. "This is the nurse from St Anne's again. "I'm calling to tell you your mother passed away about 10 minutes ago. She wasn't alone. I was with her holding her hand. She just peacefully passed on." Dead silence. I was stunned. I said, "What happened?"

I thanked her for calling. Joan and I just stood there looking at each other in disbelief. Just then, my other daughter, Sharon called. I said very softly and with reverence, "Sharon, Grandma died." She said "What?" I tried to speak a little louder and still be respectful. "Grandma died!" She said "Mom, speak up I can hardly hear you." I shouted, "Grandma is dead."

Well, you know what happened then? Joan and I started laughing because I had shouted "Grandma's dead." Sharon said, "Oh my God" and then she started to laugh because we were laughing. When I related the story of the nurse's call and what she must have thought of my insensitivity, we started to laugh even harder. After several minutes of sidesplitting laughter and a half-a-box of tissues for our tears, we began to settle down and think of what we had to do next.

First we split a beer, then I called my older brother, he knows how to take charge and get things done. He and I picked out a casket and made funeral arrangements several months before. Maybe he saw this coming, but I was totally oblivious. We thought she had come to her end several times before, as you read, maybe I thought she would never really die. Maybe it was like the boy that cried wolf. As I said, that's the way we get and got through, laughing it away. It's worked for us.

Lest you think ill of my darling children: Sharon took my Mom and Dad to Beef Carver every Sunday for years. Joan used to meet them at the library on her lunch hour, and Joan and I always planted the flowers that the others gave her for Mother's Day. These are just a few of the things my children did for and with my Mom. She was a very lucky grandma!

Aeroplane Stories
(Off we go into the wild blue yonder)

Flying to Montauk

I have lots of airplane stories. Once in 1987, after a five-day visit with my sister Joan in New Hampshire, I planned on flying to Long Island to meet my son and stay with his family for a week. They were at a camp site at Hither Hill State Park in Montauk. It was right on the ocean, a beautiful place and an annual vacation spot for them.

I packed up my things, loaded them into Joan's car and off we went to the airport. I trusted my sister (and my brother-in-law) they were both very responsible adults, so I assumed Joan knew my departure time and the time required to get from her house to the airport before the flight. Well, I was wrong.

Joan and I were talking and laughing and enjoying our ride together. As we approached the small airport and were driving alongside the runway, Joan looked over at me and said in a matter-of-fact voice, "Dee, there goes your plane." I said, "What, you mean I've missed my plane? What am I going to do now?"

She took me to the terminal; and as I said, it was a small airport that just took short flights to local destinations. She helped me out of the car, gave me my bag and said, "I have to get back, you can call Tom and figure out a way to meet up!!!"

OMG, now what am I going to do? The next flight wouldn't be for a couple of hours. Well, of course, Tom had no idea I had missed the plane. He was waiting at MacArthur airport expecting to see me. He had the kids with him who were excited to see Gramma, but now they were getting fussy. My plane had landed but I wasn't on it. They were totally confused so back to the campgrounds they went—a one-hour and thirty minute ride each way.

You've noticed the date 1987, NO CELL PHONES. I got on the next flight and finally arrived at Douglas MacArthur airport on Long Island; and of course, no Tom! I should try to call Tom but I wasn't sure of the official name of the campgrounds. How would they ever find him, and if they did, I wouldn't know what he was going to do? Luckily for me he didn't say, "The heck with her, she can just stay there till I get there, whenever that is." By then I thought to myself, I give up, I'm at the mercy of the Gods! I know what to do when that happens—take control. So, I went over to the counter and bought a pack of cigarettes (even though I had quit smoking long ago). Then I sauntered over to the bar, climbed up on the stool and ordered a beer. There was a bowl of popcorn on the bar—free—that was a bonus. What else did I need? I figured someone would find me sooner or later, so I might as well relax and enjoy myself.

Tom did eventually find me after calling his sister in Berkeley, Michigan who then called her aunt in New Hampshire and so on down the line. Of course, by then the word was out, everyone was calling everyone else, back and forth. "Where's Mom?" Actually, I never really worry too much; my kids are really smart and resourceful. I always figured they would find me in the end—if they wanted to!

Tom finally found me at the bar and we drove to the campgrounds. We spent the rest of the week walking the beach looking for shells, singing around the campfire, watching movies out on the grounds, cooking at our tent, carrying water from the pump, and trying not to touch the side of the tent when it rained. Spending time with family and especially grandkids is one of my favorite things to do.

Flying from England

Joan, James, and I went to England to visit Carol and her family, Mark and Tait. James was about ten years old at the time, I think. When we arrived, Mark, Carol's husband suggested we take the train from Great Britain under the *English Channel* to France! We hadn't been there before and we were delighted. Mark is great to travel with; he's been around a lot and makes a great travel guide.

88   A Charmed Life

We visited many of the tourist highlights, the *Cathedral of Notre Dame*, the *Eiffel Tower* (Mark and the boys had to climb to the top, of course). Carol, Joan, and I waved from below on good old terra firma. We saw the *Arc de Triomphe*; and of course, we went to the *Louvre* to see the infamous *Mona Lisa*. She smiled her smile at us—it was a fabulous trip. Our trip ended a few days later and we were off to Gatwick airport for the long flight home—Joan, James and I. After customs, we boarded our plane and settled into our seats; the three of us together with James in the middle. We were near the front so we could observe the passengers as they boarded the plane.

There was one passenger who stood out; he appeared to be from the Middle East. He was wearing a long-white garment and a small, white pill box hat. He had a black mustache and short, black beard. He stood out somewhat because his clothing was unusual garb for a man travelling to America in 1996.

After a couple of hours into our flight, we began to hear some commotion about six rows behind us. The man in the unusual garb began talking loud and disturbing the other passengers. The hostess politely asked him to please refrain from such boisterous outbursts. People were starting to move away from him to find other seats where possible. We all thought perhaps he had been drinking.

After a few warnings, to no avail, the co-pilot came out from the cockpit and again a little more forcefully asked him to settle down. By this time, he was yelling and thrashing around. We were afraid to walk past him to use the bathroom, but finally I had to take James. So, I had my arms hovering around him for protection just in case.

Soon, this character began to stand up and shout, "I'm asking God to crash this plane and kill everyone on board." The hostess and co-pilot were trying to restrain him when we heard on the loud speaker from the Pilot, "Ladies and gentleman we're going to make an emergency landing in Newfoundland. Just stay in your seats till we are on the ground. We'll give you additional directions at that time. Please just stay calm everything is under control."

We were all scared and looking at each other and speculating about what was going to happen. When we landed, we could see three police cars with flashing lights pull right up beside our plane. The flight attendant hurried us off the plane. We exited down a ramp and they directed us to a low slung building made of cinder block. We were all hanging on to our things and running for dear life. We were not at a terminal it just seemed to be a cement yard, almost like a school yard. I'm not sure where we were, we all huddled in this building looking out the windows.

After we were all off, the police boarded the plane; and in a few minutes, they led the suspect out with his hands cuffed behind his back. He had policemen all around him. They put him in the back seat of a Patrol car and drove off. Soon, we were all paraded back to the plane. We climbed the steps, found our seats, and buckled up. Everyone was speculating and talking about the "terrorist." I don't know who coined that term; it was a new word to us in America at that time.

They announced that there was not a bomb on the evicted passenger and that we were all safe. We would resume our flight home safely. Everyone was talking and some said, "Well, he didn't have a bomb on his person, but what about his luggage?" More fodder for speculation. We did arrive home safely but a little shaken up. As usual, when my friends asked me about my trip, I recited my usual mantra, "You won't believe what happened to us," but they're used to me having some outrageous story or strange experience. Actually, I don't think they really believe me; these stories are too bizarre to be true. What do you think? But again, I have *A Charmed Life*.

BC # One

I'm surprised at how naive I am at times. I seem to have missed some part of growing up and being in the real world.

Around 1992, a couple of days after having a mammogram, I got a call from the nurse. She said she saw something on my X-ray that looked suspicious. I made an appointment with a surgeon and went in for a biopsy.

He returned after the procedure, while I was still on the gurney, put his hand on my shoulder, and with a soft voice said, "Mrs. Trainor, I am sorry to tell you this, but you have breast cancer." My son, Barney had taken me to the appointment; he was so quiet and looked scared. I said, "That can't be, I am in excellent health." See how naive I am? You can be in excellent health and still get the disease. I was angry and began reciting my litany of bad words.

The doctor said, "As soon as you can make an appointment, we can do a lumpectomy. You'll also receive radiation therapy and we'll take it from there." Remember this was in the nineties. There wasn't much awareness of breast cancer like there is now. They didn't have Susan B. Komen walks for the cure or anything like that, or at least I hadn't heard much about it. I didn't even know anyone who had cancer. When I returned to work the next day, I told the school nurse and got permission from the Principal to take some time off.

The news spread like wildfire, and throughout the day different staff members came down to my room to express their concern and offer support. I was surprised at all this and did not think much about it. What was all the fuss about? *Ignorance is Bliss.* I think I must have some kind of safety mechanism because the enormity of the situation just didn't seem to sink in.

It was right before Christmas when I got the diagnosis. Remember the warning of Shakespeare's Soothsayer *Beware the*

Ides of March? Well, I say to myself, beware of Christmas tide for me and my family. Christmas seems to be a bad time for us; Joan and Carol both lost their husbands around Christmas and now this (Although Barney was born on Christmas eve so that was a good thing).

The lumpectomy was performed by Dr. Harold Wilson, a wonderful surgeon and a gentle, caring man. My incision was only three-inches long and covered with a flat bandage. In those days, they took out about twelve lymph nodes from the armpit before surgery to test them to be sure the cancer hadn't spread to the lymphatic system. After that procedure, a tube was inserted into the incision to drain the fluid which was taped to my side to empty into a plastic bag just below my hip. This apparatus had to be worn for about a week, I think. Well, here comes Barney's birthday on Christmas Eve. Since he never really got to celebrate his special day properly as a child, now as an adult, he always plans a dinner and evening out on the town inviting family and friends to come along—there were usually 8 to 10 of us. Was I going to let breast cancer get in the way of that party? Not on your life! I was one of the revelers.

Well, I had my surgery a few days before the big event, and what I did was wrap the tube around my waist and tucked the bag in the waistband of my pants near the front. I pulled the zipper up, put on a black sequin sweater to match the festive occasion, and off I went. That year we met at Alban's, a nice local restaurant. We had a wonderful time. I hope this isn't too grisly to read, or as they say, "more information you need to know." Anyway, I received seven weeks of radiation which was the standard treatment back then; and the only problem I had was my hair wouldn't hold a curl. I went to work in the morning and then to Beaumont hospital after school for treatment. However, I must say that I never felt like I belonged there. All the patients were women and who were sitting in rows of straight chairs in the waiting room talking about their cancer, their treatments and recurrences. I never sat with this group. I just continually walked around, down the hall looking into rooms going through doors. I suppose it was a nervous reaction for me because I am a walker, I walk a lot. The nurse kept directing me back to where I was supposed to be, but I never identified with the cancer patients.

I just continued on with my life working during the day and indulging my passions at night. In order of pleasure, they are: family, wallyball, volleyball, roller skating, aerobics, painting, and walking.

After my treatment ended my daughter, Carol who lived in England at the time, asked me to come for a visit. Wonderful, I can't wait... Carol and Mark picked me up at Heathrow airport. After hugs all around, Carol said to me, "Guess what? We are going to Ireland." Oh wonderful, my first visit to the Emerald Isle. "When are we going"? I asked. Carol said, "right now." As Carol and I were chatting and catching up on all the news, off we went—across the UK and down through Wales. At one point, Mark said we are passing the *Ring of Kerry*, a real tourist attraction. What a beautiful blur. One thing about my son-in-law, he only drives at one speed—High Speed! Every once in a while Mark, a rugby player would break into a bawdy drinking song, "sing along mates", he would shout. What fun!

Despite the breakneck pace, we reached the docks of Wales just in time to see our ship pull away from the moorings. We had literally missed the boat. What a disappointment, but all was not lost. Mark went to the office and learned the next ferry was the following morning at 8:00am. What could we do? Cars were already lining up for the next departure. We did all we could do—got in line and prepared to sleep in the car for the night. I got a couple of sweaters out of my suitcase for Carol and me. Mark had an old horse blanket in the boot (we call it a trunk). So we curled up, got comfy, tried to stay warm and fell asleep. Thank goodness I had jet lag so I was out like a light. In the morning, the ferry arrived right on time. We drove into the hull and lined up with all the other cars.

We went up on deck for breakfast; and although it looked like breakfast, it tasted like cardboard. Good thing the Irish breeze was invigorating, it made up for everything. Once we landed and found our "hotel", we got dressed and went out to see Dublin. The hotel was one the rugby players used, but the price was right and the ambiance was an unexpected treat.

Good Bye Dad

As you know, my ex-husband was absent for most of my children's growing-up years. When we parted ways, Jack was only twelve years old and Joan was only two. However, in their adult years, we saw him occasionally as he lived in Royal Oak some of the time, which was not far from our home. We always invited him to holiday dinners, cook-outs and birthday celebrations.

A few years ago, he discovered he had cancer and didn't have long to live; this was very sad news. Barney was the one who usually took Dad to the doctor, so he got the news first and informed the rest of the family.

Of course, the family (the kids) stepped up and took over, they made arrangements for Hospice to come in and be there for Dad "24 hours" a day. The last couple of weeks they took turns being sure one of them was there every day. They cleaned his apartment, brought him food, and although Dad couldn't hear much, they were just there for him—they gave him comfort and support. Then one day, Hospice called to let us know that the end was near.

Barney was there first just before Dad passed and soon Joan and Carol arrived, then Jack. They all stopped what they were doing and raced over to Dad's apartment as soon as they got the message. They stood around Dad's bed and tried to give him a sip of water, but he was too weak to take drink.

Barney was holding Dad's hand when he took his last breath. He was crying and saying, "Dad, don't leave, Dad, don't go." I'm sure these words have been on Barney's lips for fifty years, and yet he was never able to express them.

Sharon arrived soon after; the girls were crying. The Hospice worker called the police to confirm the death and prepared the body. Barney picked out Dad's clothes while Jack settled up with the Hospice worker. He expressed our appreciation for the wonderful work they had done. Then, he got in touch with Paul Connell at Vasu-Lynch Funeral home. He made arrangements to have Dad picked up and later cremated. Tom flew in from New Jersey the next day. Pete was in Alabama and was unable to come back.

We had a small memorial service with just the family. The girls made a picture board with photos of Dad at his family's cottage when he was about three years old. There were shots of him standing next to his first car. Also, a number of scenes from the bar, Trainor's Tavern on Woodward Avenue in Royal Oak—Dad's pride and joy. It was across from the Detroit Zoo and Hedges Wigwam. This was before Rt. 696 expressway claimed the sacred site.

At the funeral home, the music of Glen Miller's Band played softly in the background. Paul Connell gave a short eulogy, and asked if anyone wanted to say a few words. I said I wanted to say something, much to the chagrin of my kids. They always say, "There she goes again", but when I saw the picture board, it was apparent that Dad never really had "family" growing up. He couldn't give what he never had.

This tells you something about my children after their Dad left them. He was never there to support them financially or emotionally, but at the end of the day, they were there for him. They are an example to the world of charity and forgiveness.

After the service, we went out to lunch. We then resumed our regular lives. A few weeks later, Barney picked up the ashes. He didn't want to keep them at his house for long, so after considering our options, we decided to bury them at the Trainor family plot. Dad always said he wanted to be buried with his parents, so we made a plan to meet at Holy Sepulcher cemetery the following Sunday morning. We were going to plant some flowers along with the ashes. Sharon and I followed the map, over the bridge, past the sculpture of the Sacred Heart of Jesus, then around the bend to the weeping willow tree, then straight ahead.

We drove up at the same time as Joan and Carol; you wouldn't believe the sight that met our eyes. There on a low mound next to the Trainor plot, Barney and Kevin were waiting for us. They had spread out a large plaid blanket. In the center, were a big bowl of potato chips and pretzels and a tray of three different kinds of cheese with an array of mixed crackers. Off to the side was a cooler full of beer and next to that a boom box blaring out Irish music. Everyone got on their hands and knees and began digging a trough about 4 inches deep around the plot. Barney followed with the ashes. They gently planted the flowers and covered the lot with fresh top soil. Marigolds and ageratum—purple and gold—the colors were beautiful. After we watered the beds with our sprinkling can, put our tools away and cleaned up, it was time to claim our reward: cheese, pretzels, chips and beer. We did a few Irish jigs for good measure; this was our version of an Irish wake. We were laughing and having a great time. Dad would have wanted it that way.

Addendum:

I read this story to my writers' group and they asked if this was about "My Dad." Then I understood the confusion. No, this wasn't about my Dad. It seems that after some unpleasant experiences with a person, it would be hard to call them by their name. Even that familiarity brings up feelings of vulnerability. It was just easier to call him "Dad" like the kids. Even though he wasn't much of a Dad to them, that's what they always called him, Dad.

Another addendum:

The "Eagles", a fraternal organization that Dad belonged to and attended regularly, were having a memorial service to honor him at the Club. Sharon said they wanted us to come; it was a pot-luck dinner. The Director spoke fondly of Dad and said how much he would be missed. Dad was very well liked there, he had lots of friends. He was always number one on the shuffle board team and always tops at the pool table.

I showed up along with five of the kids and several grandchildren. They introduced each one of us and apparently no one knew Dad had a family. They were very surprised, doesn't that seem strange?

Public Enemy Number One

I've had my brushes with the law as you read in previous stories. But I'm usually on the right side of the law. However, one summer that all changed. I am now Birmingham's public enemy number one.

It all started innocently enough. Probably lots of crimes start that way. Then everything goes awry. Or as they say, "everything went to hell in a hand basket." But I still maintain my innocence. Let me tell you want happened and you can be the judge.

I needed mats for six drawings that I wanted to frame. I went uptown to a business that used to be called "Great Frame Up", where I always went. I discovered a new owner. She said she would be glad to help me. Together we chose the shade and texture of each mat and she proceeded to measure each picture—the outer dimension and then the inside window.

She was very friendly and seemed happy to have a customer at the "new" establishment. Within a week, I received a phone call telling me my mats were ready for pickup. Great! I picked them up and brought them home. I had all of the material laid out on my workspace ready to go. I had the foam core backing, glass, ruler, hooks, double sided tape and so on. After cutting the foam core backing, I discovered the measurements of the mats didn't correspond with the drawings. As I checked and measured each picture twice over again, I realized not one mat was correct. Yikes!

I was baffled and wondered how this could be. I saw her measure each one. I packed all six pictures up, along with the mats, and the next day I went back to the shop. The owner was away and her friend was minding the store. She pre-measured each one and confirmed my conclusion that each mat was incorrect. She said she wasn't authorized to do anything about it. She wrote me a note to give to the proprietor explaining her findings and told me to come back tomorrow. The next day, I returned with the mats, the proprietor was there. I had the mats and drawings with me and told her they were the wrong dimensions. I also showed her the note from her friend. I assumed she would either cut new ones or give me a refund.

Instead, she started raising her voice and telling me those were the dimensions I had asked for! She claimed it wasn't her fault they didn't fit. She explained that they cost her a lot of money and she couldn't afford to lose that much money. I reiterated that *she* had done the measuring. She then became louder and began pounding on the counter as she was yelling at me. I began to stand back and thought at one point that she was going to reach over the counter and hit me.

The whole scene began to escalate, or should I say deteriorate! She began to cry and scream louder. I think she hit a high "C" at one point. She raged on for about ten minutes. I remained calm and tried to reason with her. I was determined to stand by my ground, which I don't often do. I'm usually more inclined to back down. But I was right and deserved my money back. I told her to calm down again. She screamed, "Get out of here or I'm going to call the police." *What?* This is crazy, I thought. But she went to the phone and told the police a crazy lady was in her shop and wouldn't leave. I was stunned. I just stood there in disbelief. Within four minutes, two policemen came through the door. She was behind the counter still crying and was terribly distraught. One officer stood in front of her, and the other came to me to keep us separated. How scared would you be if you were confronted by a five foot, 115 pound, 84-year old woman with white hair?

She had calmed down but was still wiping her eyes; she proceeded to tell the officer in a soft voice what happened. I couldn't hear her words. The policeman with me asked me to describe my version of what had happened. I explained my dilemma and showed him the mats and the note from her friend. I expected for him to see how unreasonable she had been and to see that she was over reacting and should refund my money.

After about fifteen or twenty minutes, the first policeman said to me, "Come on, we're going to leave." He led the way and the other Officer followed behind me. As we got near the front door, he turned to me and said, "You're banned from this shop! Don't ever come back here again or you'll be arrested." I was stunned! He stood between the door and me. Maybe he thought I would go back in and try to get my refund after they left. He stood there until I went to my car that was parked next door on the gravel lot. Then, they got into their car and drove away.

I stood by my car for a moment, and then called my daughter, Joan who was at my house. I said again, as I've said so many times before, "Joan, you won't believe what just happened to me!" Joan is a fighter. She pulled up next to my car, with gravel flying and slammed on the brakes. She was there within ten minutes. She got out of her car. I could tell she was ready for battle. She said, "Come on Mom, we're going back in there to get your money." I said, "No, the police said I would be arrested if I ever went into that shop again." We decided to go to the police station and get the police report to see what the woman told them. That turned out to be a dead-end; there wouldn't be a report till the next day.

No one was interested in hearing about our mistreatment. I'm sure they hear every day about how unfairly people have been treated by the police. We went home very disheartened. We felt helpless and very angry. We were trying to decide what to do. Then, I said boldly, "I'll take her to small claims court!" She hasn't heard the last of me yet— the wheels of justice will win out.

I did just that. I got out the phone book and looked up under United States listings and finally found small claims court. I called for an appointment. The clerk gave me a list of things I had to do, paper's to bring, etc. They said I would receive a letter in the mail informing me of my court date.

I went to court with the note from her worker/friend and all the incorrectly cut mats. When I met with the clerk, I began to have second thoughts. I was beginning to weaken and thought this was insignificant in view of the Court's huge agenda and a minor issue I had. The Clerk quickly reminded me that I had a case and should pursue it to the end.

We took turns facing the judge and giving him our own rendition of events. She went first and I wanted to interrupt her but refrained. I kept my composure and waited patiently for my turn.

She looked different than I remembered her at the shop. She was not dressed up or professional by my measure. She said the shop was now closed and was no longer a registered business entity. I didn't know what to think. Was she afraid she was going to get sued and didn't want to have anything to do with it any longer? She reiterated her position that I received the services I had asked requested.

I was up next and gave my side of the story and presented my evidence. I was still carrying my big plastic envelope with the measured mats and the drawings I planned to frame. I must have presented my case well because the "verdict" was she would pay me $50 in compensation (this was still short of what she owed me by my estimation). Out in the lobby, she was prepared to write me a check, but the clerk said that wasn't acceptable. She would have to give me cash.

She didn't have an ATM account so she had to go to the cashier window and write a check to the Oakland County Court and then give it to me. I got to stand there and watch the whole process (I must say it was sweet!).

Driving home down Telegraph past all the detours and lane closings, I was so proud of myself I was almost in tears. Patting myself on the back I thought, here I am a little old lady sticking up for myself, going in front of a Judge and winning my case, good for me! And as I always say TYJ, *Thank you, Jesus!*

Dear Reader, here is a list of my stories. You can check off the ones you've read, and then look forward to reading the others in "A Charmed Life" Book II.

Tea For Two	☐	The Case of the Infamous	☐
Pete's Travel	☐	Wedding Gown	
Aeroplane Stories	☐	Walk across the Glacier	☐
The Tooth Fairy	☐	Painting In Italy	☐
Pete's Story	☐	Missing Mother Teresa	☐
Busted at the Dime Store	☐	Mom's Last Day	☐
Birthing House	☐	Kennedy Shot	☐
Ham and Cheese	☐	Dave and I at the Porn Shop	☐
Bonnie and Clyde	☐	Pete's House Fire	☐
BC #1	☐	The Easter Bunny	☐
Foster Parent	☐	BC #2	☐
Jack's Dream Car	☐	Good Bye Dad	☐
Slow Burn	☐	Carol, Mark, and I sleep	☐
Motherhood	☐	together in CA	
Married Housing - MSU	☐	Public Enemy # One	☐
Queen Of Hearts	☐	Living with the Hippies	☐
A Charmed Life	☐	We Lose Mark	☐
Joan and Mike's Wedding	☐	Hiking the Grand Canyon	☐
More Aeroplane Stories	☐	We Lose Mike	☐
ADC	☐	Joan's Pregnancy	☐
		St. Vincent de Paul's Angels	☐